PRAISE FOR ALAN DOYLE'S
A NEWFOUNDLANDER IN CANADA

"Newfoundland's streets and highways are as random and surprising as the man himself. Maybe his routes are his roots. What amazes me is, for all he has seen and done, Alan Doyle has never put another human being down. You won't be able to put him down either. You will get lost on his account. Lost on a brilliant journey in a remarkable book."   —Ron MacLean, host of *Hockey Night in Canada*
and author of *Hockey Towns* and *Cornered*

"Doyle has an eye for details, an ear for a good story and a well-honed ability to play out a yarn of his own. . . . *A Newfoundlander in Canada* entertains, providing a few comfortable hours in the thrall of a pretty great storyteller and a warm and cozy feeling about the Canada in which you live."   —*Atlantic Books*

"[*A Newfoundlander in Canada*] is a fun step-by-step trip from tightly packed tiny taverns to concerts for thousands and all the bumpy road gigs in-between."
—*The Vancouver Sun*

"A laugh-riot kitchen party on wheels that will make you fall in love with Canada all over again. Alan Doyle's heart is as big as his talent."
—Denise Donlon, media executive and author
of *Fearless as Possible (Under the Circumstances)*

"Doyle's effortless storytelling will have you on his side from the first page. He writes like he sings: with a sincerity and a love of life that is infectious. As you read this book, you'll fall in love with Canada for the first time again, even if you've lived here all your life. *A Newfoundlander in Canada* is like the country itself—much bigger than you first realize and filled to the brim with optimism, laughter, and wide-eyed wonder. As we say in Newfoundland, 'it's wicked.'"
—Mark Critch, comedian and cast member
on *This Hour Has 22 Minutes*

"[A] laugh-out-loud, insightful, heartwarming, and enjoyable tale of [Doyle's] first journey across Canada. . . . His curiosity and enthusiasm to explore the country is contagious, and allows us to see snippets of Canada through his eyes almost as though we were seeing it ourselves for the first time."

—*Winnipeg Free Press*

ALAN
DOYLE

A NEWFOUNDLANDER IN CANADA

ANCHOR CANADA

Library and Archives Canada Cataloguing in Publication

Doyle, Alan, 1969-, author
A Newfoundlander in Canada / Alan Doyle.

Issued in print and electronic formats.
ISBN 978-0-385-68621-1 (softcover).—ISBN 978-0-385-68620-4 (EPUB)

1. Doyle, Alan, 1969-. 2. Musicians—Newfoundland and Labrador
—Biography. 3. Great Big Sea (Musical group). 4. Autobiographies.
I. Title.

ML420.D755A3 2018   782.42164092   C2017-902473-6

Book design: Kelly Hill
Cover photos: (front) Vanessa Heins; (back) Shehab Illyas

Interior images: (compass, plane, confused man) *Adcuts of the 20s and 30s*, Dover
Publications, Inc.; (guitar case, knife and fork) *3800 Early Advertising Cuts*, Dover
Publications, Inc.; (cat) *Scan This Book*, Art Direction Book Company; (Mary and Jesus)
The Complete Encyclopedia of Illustration, Grammercy Books; (dinosaur, maple leaf, rope)
Clipart.com; (cod) #113753, *Zoology of New York*, New York Public Library Digital
Collections; (stick man) Alan Doyle

Printed and bound in the USA

Published in Canada by Anchor Canada,
a division of Random House of Canada Limited,
a Penguin Random House Company

www.penguinrandomhouse.ca

10 9 8 7 6 5 4 3 2 1

Penguin
Random House
ANCHOR CANADA

For Joanne and Henry

CONTENTS

ix   *Author's Note*

ı   *A Map of Canada*

9   Home

27   Nova Scotia

51   The Purple Dinosaur

57   Prince Edward Island

73   Worst Seat Ever

87   New Brunswick

97   Supper

107   Quebec

119   Language

125   Ontario 1

137   Canada Day 1997

153   Ontario 2

163   Ralph on Ice

169   Manitoba

185   Fred's

191   Saskatchewan

201   Cat in the Culvert

207   Alberta

221   Fort Mac Bus

227   British Columbia

237   Home Again

243   *Acknowledgements*

AUTHOR'S NOTE

This is a memoir. What follows in these pages is a collection of my memories. I cast my mind's eye back to the times described here, and this is what I see. I can almost guarantee you that I am the only one who remembers it all like this.

I have changed the names of some people and places to protect those who may not want to be identified here. For the same reason, there are situations that involved a few people but are presented as having happened to me alone. But I have intentionally invented no one, nowhere, and nothing in this book.

Thanks so much for reading.

Alan

A MAP OF CANADA

There once was a boy who lived in a tiny fishing village on an island in the middle of the ocean. That boy was me. And there on the old new bridge separating the Catholic and Protestant sides of Petty Harbour, I daydreamed about what else might be waiting for me over the tall hills surrounding my tiny home.

I would lie awake at night in the modest bedroom I shared with my brother, Bernie, and wonder aloud, as he muttered sleepy responses.

"How dark does it get in the desert?"

"Real dark, probably. Go to sleep."

"Is a skyscraper taller than Boone's Head?"

"Don't know. Never saw one. Go to sleep, please."

"Can you drive from New York to Los Angeles?"

"Yes, saw it on TV. Go to friggin' sleep."

"How far is that?"

"Don't know. Shut up and go to sleep."

"Denny said there are mountains so high in India that you can look down on a plane. Is that true?"

"Yep."

"So how far away is Vancouver?"

"Don't know. I'm asleep."

I confess that as a very young fella I spent an equal amount of time thinking about Dublin and Hollywood as I did about Toronto or Vancouver. To me, they were all the same, faraway places that I had little, if any, chance of ever seeing in person. I was probably supposed to be more familiar with Calgary than Lisbon, but I wasn't. I had met lots of people from Portugal, as the White Fleet often summered off the rocks in Petty Harbour buying excess fish from the locals, but I don't think I'd ever met anyone from Alberta.

For a while what country I was part of was not entirely clear to me. Most of the older people in Petty Harbour said we were still part of the country of Newfoundland and therefore I was a Newfoundlander. My mom and teachers said we were a part of Canada and therefore I was a Canadian. I was certainly happy with either one. Standing on the bridge in Petty Harbour, I could have been part of Canada, China, Poland, or South Africa and it would not have made one pinch of difference to my day-to-day. They all seemed equally distant and fantastical to me.

But the truth, of course, is that my mom and teachers were right. I was a Canadian. The Dominion of Newfoundland joined the country of Canada in 1949, when both my parents were well into their childhoods, and though I rarely think of myself as such, I am a first-generation Canadian. Though unlike other first-generation Canadians, my parents never left anywhere and arrived anywhere else. So here we all were supposedly in a new country. A new country we knew very little about and one that probably knew very little about us.

Sometime in my earliest years of school, I was given a photo-copied map of Canada pasted onto a piece of construction paper. There were no words or lines to separate provinces, just an out-line of the mainland of the country and its outlying islands. My job was to take my crayons and cover it with as many details as I could name—cities, lakes, mountains, landmarks, even buildings of note. I had very little to go on except for what I'd heard the adults around me describe. With the voices of my parents and of other grown-ups around Petty Harbour in my head, I began to fill in the map. As far as I knew the map of Canada consisted of the following regions from east to west.

First, I wrote NEWFOUNDLAND in the ocean by the funny-shaped island reaching backwards to the mother country of Ireland or England, depending on which side of the bridge you were from. I knew I lived only a few kilometres from the most easterly point in all of Canada and in fact North America, and if I wanted to go anywhere in the province of Newfoundland or the country of Canada, I had only one way to go.

And that was west across the overpass and the mythical yet very real gateway between rural Newfoundland and its baymen, like my young self, and the city of St. John's and its townies, like the adult self I hoped to be. So on the map of Newfoundland, I figured there could be only two regions. In crayon I spelled out in capital letters the one around the greater St. John's area known as TOWN, and the rest would be a giant area known as AROUND THE BAY.

I knew Labrador was a place up above me, but the fishermen on the wharf referred to going there as "down on the Labrador," which I found, and still find, confusing. In the same vein, folks from my hometown would say "let's go up the Southern Shore." I have never heard a single person outside of Newfoundland, before or since, say "down to the north" as in Labrador or "up to the south" as in the Southern Shore. No wonder my mapping skills were stunted so early. But I knew Labrador was actually a part of my province, and not part of Quebec, the province to which it is attached, which again was very confusing. All I really knew about Labrador was that it was a vast, beautiful, sparsely populated place with a huge coastline and massive rivers and an iron ore mine in Labrador City. I had heard a cousin say you could drive from Labrador City to a town in Quebec in twenty minutes or so, but I honestly thought that was just a story. "Imagine!" I once said to the other ten-year-olds working on the wharf in Petty Harbour. "Driving from one province to another and back while on your dinner break. Must be impossible."

So with my crayon I mapped out Labrador as a mass of land along the mainland coast above Newfoundland that for some reason bent inland just long and far enough to reach Labrador City and the mine. I asked my teacher why the Labrador–Quebec border bent in so sharply. Walking briskly up the aisle, she told me, "Because that is where the mine is." I asked, "Why didn't Quebec get the mine?" She broke her stride and turned her head to the side and appeared to be thinking about it, and after a little while she turned back to me and said, "Finish your work now." I wrote LABRADOR down the coastline.

For the first years of my life I was sure we were part of the Maritimes, but it turns out we are not. We are part of Atlantic Canada, which comprises the Maritimes and Newfoundland and Labrador. Not sure who was in charge of that distinction, but even as a kid it seemed unnecessary to me. So I drew a big circle around Nova Scotia, Prince Edward Island, and New Brunswick and wrote MARITIMES in the ocean between them, then set to try to name what I knew about them individually.

I'd heard an uncle say he drove a cement truck onto the ferry on the west coast of Newfoundland and when it landed on the other side he was in North Sydney. So I wrote NORTH SYDNEY in what I would come to learn was Cape Breton Island and drew an arrow to its northernmost tip, as I figured that's where the ferry would land. Turns out I was off by quite a bit, as the NL–NS ferry bypasses about 180 kilometres of Nova Scotia land before finally docking about halfway down Cape Breton Island.

I knew there was a city where many of the airplanes headed our way stopped, so I just wrote HALIFAX across the lower part of Nova Scotia.

I knew Prince Edward Island was the little bit in the bay next to HALIFAX. To make the label fit, I used the province's initials, but in my haste, I put PIE there instead. My teacher thought that was hilarious. (I was delighted many years later when my own son asked if we could go see one of the sandy beaches on P.I.E.)

I knew there was something between PIE and Quebec, but was not sure what it was. All I could recall was how people from St. John's area complained their Sears catalogue packages were always being sent to a city with almost exactly the same name in another Atlantic province. I figured this must be the place, so in the New Brunswick area, I wrote OTHER ST. JOHNS.

As a Montreal Canadiens fan, I knew the next bit quite well. I wrote MONTREAL, QUEBEC, which I'm sure must have spilled over into Ontario. I drew the Habs logo, the H inside the C, somewhere in the middle of the province as an homage to the team I loved so much.

I knew the Maple Leafs came from the next place to Montreal as they played each other on *Hockey Night in Canada* quite often. I knew about the CN Tower because the just-built tallest building in the world that looked like a fancy robot was on TV a lot too. But I knew this city for many reasons besides.

You see, Toronto—pronounced "Chronto" in Petty Harbour—was the place where everybody went to for seemingly everything. They went there to work in factories, to catch planes, to go on holidays, and to watch hockey games at the Gardens. Every few weeks there would be a card game or a darts tournament to raise money to send someone from Petty Harbour to Toronto for a kidney transplant, or to see a specialist about a bone disorder, or for heart surgery, or any myriad of ailments not easily or quickly treated in Newfoundland. There were so many people going there for so many different reasons, I assumed it must be a huge place. I knew around where it started, but had no idea where it ended. So on the crayon map, as I could not recall how the city was spelled on the Maple Leafs jersey, I wrote in the name the way it sounded. I wrote CHRONTO through all of Ontario and what must have been most of Manitoba.

I skipped over to the other coast and wrote BRITISH COLUMBIA up and down next to the Pacific Ocean. I knew there was a city called VANCOUVER in there somewhere, so I wrote that right beneath the BRITISH COLUMBIA, and as I saw people skiing there on TV, I drew mountains, quite coincidentally exactly where the Rockies separate B.C. and Alberta.

There were still two massive pieces of unnamed land. I strained to recall conversations the adults would have about where people went to find work and all I could think was Chronto. Then I remembered a series of chats on the wharf between two fishermen cursing the low price for fish and the high price of gas.

"Sure you'd starve to death at this racket. Jaysus, we're spending more than we're making. Me and the brother are going out

West to see if we can make a go of it. If it don't work there, shag it, we'll go up north and give it a go."

"Out West" and "up north." I figured that must be what was left.

I wrote OUT WEST over Saskatchewan and Alberta, and across the top of the map, from Alaska to Hudson Bay, I wrote UP NORTH.

That was it. That was all I knew about the country my mom and teachers told me was mine and most of the older fishermen on the wharf told me was not. Outside of my own province, I wrote about ten names and drew one tower and a mountain range and a Habs logo. At that tender age, that was my Canada.

How did Newfoundland fit into Canada? Did we fit at all? I wasn't sure, and I supposed it did not really matter all that much to me because there was almost no chance I'd ever get to see it anyway.

Then, in the final days of 1992, my life changed forever, when Séan McCann shook my hand on Water Street and asked me to join a band that he and Bob Hallett and Darrell Power were destined to start. A few weeks later Great Big Sea was born, and two of the biggest, most impossible dreams of my life became a whole lot more possible. I was going to play in a band for a living. And these guys were not just aiming to play around St. John's and up the Southern Shore where I'd apprenticed for so many years. These guys were talking about going across the vast island of Newfoundland en route to the country of Canada. And these boys were serious. We were going "up to Canada," as my grandfather would say. I could not have been more excited.

HOME

"The wipers are broke, so we're using Bob's belt and a rope I found by Paddy's Pond to pull them back and forth. Works pretty good, hey?"

Darrell is shouting out the open window of his eight-year-old green Honda Civic hatchback, headed west through the driving rain on the Trans-Canada just outside of St. John's. He occasionally wipes his glasses with his finger so he can see through the drops. Bob is in the passenger seat, with his window open as well, his wiry Irish-red locks getting wetter and wetter with every second. I can see through the matted ginger hair just enough to know how pissed he is by this development. While he's pulling the belt and wipers to his side of the windshield, Darrell releases the rope, and then they switch and repeat like two mad oarsmen on a crazy jerry-built ship pushing headlong into a storm bound for God Knows Where.

"Ha! Yes, b'y!" Séan's face is dangerously close to Darrell's. Séan and I are in a different car, his nine-year-old Ford Festiva hatchback, driving the same direction on the same highway in the same rain in the lane next to our bandmates. Séan is shouting out the open window at Darrell and I am behind the wheel, driving a car with standard transmission for exactly the first time in my life.

What could possibly go wrong?

We were headed out to cross Newfoundland and back on our first-ever tour, our entire gear barely filling two small cars. Just two speakers, an audio mixing board, microphones and stands, two acoustic guitars, a bodhran, a bass, an accordion, a mandolin, a fiddle, and some tin whistles. There was much joking and carrying on as we rolled west, but in the few quiet moments, each of us had our own fantasies of a much bigger tour to come sometime in the near or distant future. Of a fleet of buses, fitted with cushy bunks for us and the crew of technicians who'd carry and tune our instruments. Of transport trucks full of sound and lighting equipment to load into the biggest concert venues in the country. Of record deals, music videos, and heartfelt acceptance speeches on televised award shows. We joked about these things like we were talking about winning the lotto, not letting on that somewhere in the bottom of our hearts and the back of our minds, we actually believed all this possible.

On a narrow highway through the centre of an island in the middle of the North Atlantic, we were bound for Stephenville, which is really as far west as you can drive for a St. John's band without getting in the ocean at Port aux Basques and making the overseas journey to Canada. Just how long a drive it is, is open to much interpretation, especially among Newfoundlanders themselves.

"Can't do it in one day. Too far," some St. John's townie would offer as direction. "You'd be killed by the moose."

"Me and Dad goes from Stephenville Crossing to town in seven hours with a load a wood on the truck," another fella might say. "Don't even stop to piss."

I don't think I've ever heard anyone say that Gander is 323 kilometres from St. John's. But I've heard many variations of the following chat.

"We got a gig at the Flyers Club tomorrow," I'd mention after a night at a bar on George Street. "How far is it from St. John's to Gander?"

"Town to Gander? Oh, yer knocking the arse off three and a half hours, I s'pose," one patron would suggest.

"Three and a half hours to Gander!" his buddy would counter. "What, are ya walking with your back broke? I gets there in two forty-five with the new radar scanner."

"Depends on if you got good tires," a third would advise. "You won't get past the Doe Hills with bologna skins on."

"What?" Someone else might be disgusted by the notion. "Snow tires'll do you no good when the rain is blowing up between the cut in the hills. If you wants to get to Gander before supper, you better leave before noon. And that's a fact."

And on it would go. That was as close to reliable directions and drive-time estimates as you could expect to get in the early nineties in Newfoundland.

Regardless, rain or no rain, wipers or no wipers, for somewhere between the next six and twenty-six hours, we were rolling in tandem across the sixteenth-biggest island in the world to play the first gig of our first tour.

As the road turns onto a rare straightaway and I feel confident enough to glance away from the wet white and yellow lines, I look across at my friends, my travel companions, my band. Séan McCann, Bob Hallett, and Darrell Power have been playing in some combination together in the vibrant pub scene of downtown St. John's since the late eighties. They had formed two bands, the Newfoundland Republican Army and the very successful Rankin Street, and were the undisputed kings of the circuit. As the story goes, Séan saw me playing at a few bars around downtown and figured I would be a good match. A few handshakes and many songs later, we were walking onstage at Memorial University in front of a thousand or so revellers at our first-ever gig.

Building on the foundation of the boys' years of work, I jumped aboard a train that already had quite a head of steam. Within weeks, Great Big Sea was the hottest thing in the St. John's scene. Very quickly I came to learn that the boys' individual skill sets offstage were almost as valuable as their onstage talents.

Séan McCann had a voice that soared above most other men's and in fact started where mine ended. He was great on the bodhran, that Celtic goat-skinned hand drum, and could strum a guitar with amazing percussion. He was a poet, too, and could stitch words together in beautiful and compelling ways.

Offstage, he was the best salesman I'd ever seen. He could get the club to pay us 10 per cent more than we expected and get a brewery to sponsor the night to boot. He had adopted the catch-phrase from an older, more seasoned club veteran around town: "If there's only one crowd paying you to play the club, you're doing it wrong."

Bob Hallett's voice was lower than mine and his thick Corner Boy townie accent made him difficult to understand when speaking. It often took people weeks if not months to tune in to his turn of phrase. During a video shoot for "Goin' Up," our long-time photographer and Ontario native Andrew came to me in front of the old rickety shed we were to climb. "Al, what is Bobber saying about not wanting a dog or something?" I just looked at Andrew until he offered more explanation. "He keeps saying he doesn't want a ruff or something?" I thought about it for a second and then tried to translate Ontario mainlander back into Corner Boy townie. "Andrew, did Bob say something like, 'I tell you one bloody thing, you won't be getting me on da friggin' ruff today'?" Andrew nodded. "He means roof," I explained to him. "It just sounds like 'ruff' in Corner Boy."

While some found it tough at times to understand his speech, there was no such trouble when he opened his mouth to sing. Like a classically trained baritone, he could harmonize as good as anyone I'd ever met. And just as important for the band, he picked up new instruments as easy as the rest of us picked up socks off the floor. Whatever the song wanted—a fiddle, an accordion, a mandolin, a whistle—he would learn the part on that instrument in no time at all.

Offstage, Bob was the most logical person I'd ever met. He could instantly remove emotion from any decision, a trait that would save us time and time again in the years to come. He could write a paragraph for a press release or a radio ad and make it sound so professional we'd come off as a band from the mainland coming to town for one night only, when in fact we had played the same pub two weeks earlier and the one two doors down the night before. He was meticulous and organized and had visions of the band well past the pubs of Newfoundland and Atlantic Canada.

Darrell Power did not have a naturally low voice, but he could sing bass on command. Likewise, he was quite a good guitar and mandolin player, but switched to bass to round out the sound we needed. He was a versatile musician and really the only one of us who could play rock and roll *and* folk music when the band got going.

Offstage he had, in spades, exactly what every band needs so very often: the ability to bring humour to a tense situation at the exact right moment. Just when the drive became tedious and boring, Darrell would tell the perfect joke or sing a song about some foolishness. The first time I ever heard the song "Johnny McEldoo," about a man who went on an eating binge, was during a slow and tedious drive from Gander to St. John's. Darrell figured the band needed a morale boost and just started singing, amongst other things,

> *"Johnny McEldoo turned red, white and blue*
> *As a plate of Irish stew he soon put out of sight*
> *He shouted out 'Encore!' with a roar for some more*
> *That he'd never felt before such a keen appetite.*
> *We ordered eggs and ham, bread and jam, what a cram*
> *But him, we couldn't ram, though we tried our level best*
> *For everything we brought, cold or hot, mattered not*
> *It went down him like a shot but he still stood the test"*

He seemingly had an endless supply of songs to lighten the mood. Often they'd be so ridiculous, we'd be annoyed by his first verse, but by the second or third, we'd all be singing in harmony. He was completely unfazed by flat tires, long drives, and apparently busted windshield wipers.

There's no better example of the force of nature the three of them could be than the regular Sunday night gig they landed us that first summer in 1993. 7 George was a long, narrow bar on George Street that has been renamed once or twice since. The owner wanted us to be the regular Sunday night band for the summer. He no doubt figured he would get us for a deal, as the bars had to close at midnight. Somehow, Séan convinced him to pay us our full $500 fee even though we would play only half a night. But Bob was worried about the house we would get, as we would have played just down the road the night before and maybe even that afternoon. "Why would anyone wait to see us Sunday night?" he asked in one of our many meetings.

"Talent show!" Darrell said. "I got a buddy who would come down to sing a few tunes." That was another thing about Darrell: he always had a buddy. For everything. Everywhere.

The boys loved the idea, and Séan figured we could even get a brewery to pay us to have one of their beers featured on the night. Off he went to the local branch of Labatt Brewery, who were about to launch an overproof beer called Black Ice. In that one conversation, Séan put together a deal to get us a little money, a bunch of beer for prizes on the night, and a pile of beer for us to take home or sell or do with whatever we wanted. Then he got a studio to give us recording time and an airline to give tickets to Toronto for prizes and for us.

Bob put together an ad that read like a movie trailer. "This Summer, Sunday is the hottest night on George Street with the hottest band, Great Big Sea, but the star of the show is . . . YOU! Brought to you by 7 George and Black Ice and Air Nova, a Talent Night hosted by Great Big Sea and your chance to shine."

It all came together in a day or so. The band would play one short set, and as people often wanted to sing pop or country or rock tunes, Darrell and I would serve as the house band for the evening. The combination of Darrell's versatility and affability could get even the most reluctant person to jump up and sing, and he would most likely know how to play any tune they chose from 1967 through 1988.

So Séan brokered the deal and got us paid in two or three or four different ways. Bob's promotion worked—the place was rammed from night one till the finale on week ten. Darrell's musical flexibility and good nature, along with a list of buddies as long as your arm, kept the contestants running to the stage.

The busier we got, the more organized and official the whole thing became. Bob led the charge, legitimizing the business side of the band. "We're gonna need a pot of money if a gig comes up around the bay or on the mainland, and we'll need a budget to do the CD, so we can't be divvying up piles of five-dollar bills after every gig." Within weeks we had a company, a shareholders' agreement, and a bank account where we dumped the money from the gigs. We put each other on salary, and for the remainder of 1993, the four members of Great Big Sea each made $250 a week. We saved a couple of thousand dollars over the month of April, and in May we went into Dermot O'Reilly's basement studio and knocked out our self-titled indie CD that we came to call the Blue CD. We sent it off to be mastered and mass-produced, which for us meant a whopping two thousand copies.

As the boys were so good at the sell and business end of the gigs, I figured the best thing I could do was look after our sound desk, speakers, and the rest of our equipment. Dozens of times a month, after a run at a bar, we would tear it all down and load it into my red minivan, and I'd haul the gear back to the Château de Suez, my university lodgings, where I had a large closet to store the Great Big Sea kit.

It often happened that we would play a weekend matinee in one bar on George Street and then an evening gig somewhere else on the street. "No sense loading everything into the van," I'd say. That summer it was not uncommon to see me and one or two of the fellas pushing a twenty-four-space audio rack, with a Peavey speaker balanced on top, up George Street around 6 p.m. I can still feel the bumpity-bump-bump of the casters catching in and rolling over the old cobblestones in the road, and I could not have been happier.

We'd been doing quite well in the city and figured it was time to head beyond the overpass and into the rest of Newfoundland. My van was not reliable enough for highway driving, so we decided to take Séan's and Darrell's hatchbacks instead. We had not yet reached the 20 kilometre mark when I drove up next to Bob and Darrell driving with the windows down in a rainstorm pulling the busted wipers from one side to the other with a rope and a belt.

With their previous band, Séan, Darrell, and Bob had travelled to Gander, Corner Brook, and a few of the other larger towns on the island. Bob and Séan had both travelled extensively off-island. They'd not only seen parts of North America but visited the U.K. and Ireland and parts of Europe. Darrell had been to Canada's mainland a time or two. But for all of us this would be the first multi-stop tour. We had booked the dates ourselves over the phone, with not so much as a sheet of paper in agreement about what was expected of us or how much the clubs would pay us.

But we were going anyway. So west we went.

I'd done a small part of this drive with my family, but now, with my eyes open wider than ever, I saw so many things I'd not noticed before, like the place names you pass while driving in Newfoundland. Eyeing Come By Chance on a road sign made me wonder what it must be like for a mainlander to encounter the province for the first time. Would they think we were shagging with them when they passed a Heart's Desire, a Heart's Delight, and a Little Heart's Ease in a matter of minutes? Would they giggle at or be horrified by bold white letters on a green sign announcing a Joe Batt's Arm or a Cow Head? Surely they would think us a bunch of jokesters when they noticed places like Leading Tickles and Conception Bay. And what in God's name would they think when they saw that right across from a Spread Eagle was a Dildo?

Westward-bound through the isthmus. The narrow piece of land that attached the H of the Avalon Peninsula to the main island of Newfoundland is notable for a few reasons. It is the only place in all of Newfoundland where you can, at the same time, see both Trinity Bay to the north and Placentia Bay to the south, and hence, it's the one vantage point where you know for certain you are on an island in the middle of the Atlantic. Not on the edge of it, with a continent behind you, but in the middle of it, with nowhere to retreat, even if you had to.

After nine hours and a stop at the Badger Diner, we reached our first destination in Stephenville, the Black's Motel, where we had been promised two rooms, which we decided to split by car. So Séan and I took one room, while Bob and Darrell took the other.

As the boys grabbed their bags, I paused in the parking lot to mark the occasion. I was about to stay in a hotel room on a real tour for the very first time in my life. Come to think of it, this was one of the first times I'd ever stayed in a hotel at all. My family certainly could never afford to take any kind of vacation to Florida or anywhere else for that matter. I had partied with pals in rooms on hockey or other "recreational" weekends only once or twice before, so crashing in a cot-and-sleeping-bag-filled room with six to eight fellas was the sum total of my hotel experience.

I stood there leaning on Séan's Festiva with my two feet in a pothole about two inches deep, rainwater seeping into my sneakers as I surveyed the castle that was Black's Motel. I took a breath and studied the flashing Va ancy sign. The letters that did work flashed at irregular intervals, which, intentional or not, was a cool design feature, and certainly I was not about to let a poorly attended light bulb ruin this for me.

All I could see was the luxury of it all. The narrow scratched and dented doors were located conveniently right off the parking lot. We'd be able to load our stuff right from the cars into the rooms after the gig. Brilliant. As I walked slowly into our room, I noticed the doors were also nice and thin, so you'd be able to hear everything that was going on in the parking lot and the lounge across the way. The beds were definitely big enough for more than one person, but Séan and I had the place to ourselves. The sheets were almost see-through, not like those thick flannel ones Mom gave me for our frat house in St. John's, so I knew I would not be too warm. The rotary-dial phone was right between the two beds on a handy nightstand. I opened the drawer and was surprised to see a Bible. I picked it up and flung it open, just to see which verse it would fall to, as if there would be an oracle or fortune cookie message hidden within just for me. As the Good Book fell open, I saw that many of the pages had been torn out, and torn out with purpose.

"Well used, I suppose," I said to Séan, who had a look of pleasant disbelief.

I went to check out the bathroom and was stopped mid-stride when I noticed two sinks, one on the wall in the room itself and the other inside the bathroom with the toilet and tub. Both had mirrors above them and had individually wrapped soaps in the soap holders.

"Two sinks. Two soaps, McCann!"

"Yes, b'y. Wicked. Two channels on the TV, too." Séan was already stretched out on the bed.

"Yeah, deadly. And this toilet has been . . . wait now . . ." I had to get down on my knees to read what was printed on the paper strap holding the lid and the seat together. *"Sanitized for Our Protection."* Pretty upscale, I thought.

There were two small tubular bottles of body and hair wash laid over two white facecloths and towels on the edge of the yellowish tub. I immediately took one and stuffed it in my pocket. A place as posh as this wouldn't miss that one bottle, I figured.

When I came out from the can, Séan was standing in the doorway chatting to Bob. They appeared to be all business.

"Hey, Bob," I joined in, "we can load the stuff right in here from the parking lot after the gig."

"Yes, b'y," Bob agreed, and flicked a cigarette butt in the air, his favourite punctuation to any chat. "Let's get over there and get set up. We might have time to come back for a nap before the first set."

I chucked my knapsack on the bed and we boarded our respective hatchbacks and set off for the gig, at a club called 401 Main. On our way through the town I noticed buildings left over from the massive U.S. Air Force base that had tripled Stephenville's population in the fifties and sixties. Many of the buildings had been boarded up or repurposed since the Americans left, and there was a distinct sense that this town was once much busier. A generation before, over four thousand American soldiers occupied this place, and the town was hopping. The biggest celebrities in the world had entertained here. Names like Frank Sinatra, Marilyn Monroe, Elvis Presley, and Bob Hope had graced the billboards in the not-so-distant past.

We arrived at the club at the agreed time of 4 p.m. We pulled up to the side door as instructed and gave it a quick knock that went unanswered. After a few more kicks, I walked around to the front door and found knocks at that door unanswered as well. I walked back to the lads waiting by the cars.

"I don't think anyone's here."

"Yeah, probably can't believe we're on time." I couldn't tell if Darrell was kidding or not.

After ten minutes or so, it turned out that Darrell was right. Rod, the owner of the club, rolled down the laneway and jumped out of his pickup. The other boys had a passing acquaintance with him, as they had met in St. John's a few years back, and they all winked or shook hands or waved to each other.

"Holy Jesus. A band from town on time for once. Well done, b'ys. How are ye? Is this the new fella?" He nodded to me, and the boys nodded back.

We loaded our stuff through the back door, and the first thing that struck me was the size of the club. It was huge compared to the pubs we'd been playing in downtown St. John's. It confused me that a place with one-tenth the population of St. John's would have a club four times as big as any I'd ever seen in town. As the band technician, I was worried that our tiny pub PA system would never fill this massive room. We put our two speakers on rickety stands on either side of the back corner of the wide dance floor and quickly assembled our tiny set-up of mics and instruments. We had no lights, so I went around the room pointing some of the white track lighting towards the makeshift stage. It felt strange to do so when there were dozens of high-tech disco lights installed in the ceiling of the bar. "I wish we could use some of the PA and lights," Bob worried. "Gonna be pretty small-sounding." But Rod explained they were tied in to the huge DJ system tuned around the club and only programmed for certain songs.

I tried to be optimistic, but I knew Bob's concerns were warranted.

On the way back to the hotel I spied a pizza shop called Domino. I'd heard of a massive chain restaurant in the U.S., but of course I'd never seen one. I assumed franchises from this size of company would just be in big cities, like McDonald's and Burger King are.

"You have a Domino's!" I said to the impressive desk clerk back at the hotel. "Cool."

"That's not just a Domino's, my honey. That's *our* Domino's."

Turns out the family-owned restaurant in Stephenville predated the international franchise. When they received a cease and desist order from the giant company, they flat out refused to obey it. In a resulting lawsuit, the court found in favour of the family and allowed them to use the name on their own restaurant for as long as they saw fit.

It was a brilliant illustration of Newfoundland spunk. And I loved it immediately.

"Last chance for a nap!" My chat with the stunning desk clerk was interrupted. I took the boys' advice and lay on a hotel bed that was mine and mine alone, for the first time in my life.

I'd not slept a wink when it came time to head out.

There is an anxiousness that hits when you make your way through a new town to the gig you are playing that night. No matter how much buzz there's been, no matter how many tickets have been sold or how much interest there's been online or anything else that might forecast a great turnout, you can't help but peek around to the front door hoping to see some kind of lineup. You feel completely reassured when there is one, and completely uneasy when there isn't one.

We drove by the front door of the club. There was no lineup. At all. Not one person opened or closed the door as we passed.

I walked into 401 Main at nine o'clock and it looked exactly as it had at four. Cavernous. Not a single patron had entered since the doors had opened an hour before. Our first set was to be at 9:30. We waited fifteen minutes past that, and by then there were maybe a dozen in a room that could fit hundreds. Worse again, many of them were half a mile away at the bar and not the least bit interested in us, even if our little speakers could have reached them in the back of the room. We went completely unnoticed for the entirety of the sixty-minute set. I swear the only four people that even know for sure we played at all were me, Séan, Darrell, and Bob.

After skulking around at the back door during the break, I was relieved to see a few more people had showed up by the time we went on for the second set. There were now closer to a hundred people in the room, but they were mostly all at the bar and only a few up by the stage. We ripped into our fastest and loudest stuff for those who were close enough to hear.

Some even tried to dance, but there was a problem. We were a pub band trying to play in a dance club. Dancing, in most rural Newfoundland establishments at that time, was not about positioning yourself in front of the band and letting yourself go. In places like 401 Main, dancing most often meant a man asking a woman to dance as he would have at a 1950s sock hop, spending three minutes on the floor together, and then retreating to their respective tables and stations. The clientele here were used to dancing to rock and roll and blues-inspired music, which we did not play. They were driven to the floor by the kick and snare beats of the drum kit, which we did not have.

I wish I could report that the second night was better than the first. It was barely as good. It was punctuated by a fella at the bar striding up to me after our first, unnoticed set.

"Ye fellas sounds pretty Irishy. Not that good for dancing. You do any rock and roll, like AC/DC or Zeppelin?"

What I wanted to say in return was, "Yes, b'y, we got one acoustic guitar, a bodhran, and an accordion. Of course we does dozens of metal tunes. Hold on, I'll get the mandolin and we rips off some Sabbath for you the next set." What I did say was, "I think we can do some Buffalo Springfield," as I knew Darrell could sing their big protest hit "For What It's Worth." But when we played it, buddy was chatting at the bar and went to the bathroom halfway through. Jaysus.

When the night was done we packed up our gear and Rod paid our fee as promised, though I'm sure he did not make a cent off us, and we skulked back to the motel. Back in the parking lot we figured it best to keep our instruments with us in our rooms, so we stood in the same puddle as earlier and chatted about the usual things bands talk about after they do poorly. We blamed the PA system, the foolish DJ music and lights, the inadequate staging, the people who "just didn't get it."

Without saying so, I wondered if we had what it took to go beyond George Street. There and then, I knew that if we had any chance at all, if we were to appeal to more people, we would have to be better technically and more versatile musically. And as we carried our meagre pile of equipment into our rooms, I think we all knew it.

I had the two guitar cases and Séan had a bodhran and a foot on one of Bob's tickle trunks—Bob held as much stuff of his as he could carry—and Darrell leaned on his rectangular bass case as we stood in a circle and made plans for an early leave in the morning.

Bagged and more than a little bit demoralized, I walked into the hotel room, which didn't look anywhere near as cool as it did the day before. My last sight as I closed the blinds was Séan and Darrell chatting with the rectangular bass case upright between the two of them.

The alarm woke me in the morning, and I immediately opened the blinds to let the daylight in and to keep myself awake. I didn't have my glasses on yet, but an odd shape in the parking lot caught my eye. I grabbed my specs and was not surprised to see that Darrell and Séan were not there, but very surprised to see the bass case still was, like a surviving relic of a recent battle. It was so solidly perched, I swear it would have lasted the winter there.

As I went out to get it, I wondered if it would be like Excalibur's sword and only the true of heart could move it. I prepared for the test. It moved on the first flick, which I took to mean I would be king someday.

The boys were up and ready to roll ten minutes early, and we were on the road again. These early Newfoundland runs in the first few months of the band's life would take us to Gander, Grand Falls, Corner Brook, Clarenville, and Carbonear, to Bay d'Espoir and Bay Roberts and other wonderful spots on the island. I loved the experience of exploring our home province, but I wasn't kidding myself or anyone else. I gave my all in those early Newfoundland shows, but I kept my eye firmly on the prize. And the prize was Canada. I knew that if we were to make it in the business we'd have to go abroad. I knew we had to make it there before we made it anywhere else, including home.

When we finally got the call, I felt a bit like a dog who'd caught a car. We'd landed gigs in Nova Scotia, and as we made our way to the boat, I felt sick to my stomach. An anxiety came over me like I had not felt since leaving my little house on Skinner's Hill to go to kindergarten. There was so much unknown that it overwhelmed me as we lined up for the ferry. Would they like us? Do they even know any Newfoundland traditional music? Will we get lost on the way or on the way back?

When we finally rolled aboard the massive metal boat and nestled deep in its belly, I felt even more anxious and wondered if I was claustrophobic. I wasn't. I just wanted to see Newfoundland one more time before we sailed away.

I knew this place. And it knew me. And though I dreamed of it and chased it for years, now that it was finally here, I was scared to be going to a place where neither of those things were true. As the engines roared, I twisted and wandered and made my way to the outside observation deck as the stack announced our leaving. It would take close to an hour before the Newfoundland shore disappeared into the horizon.

I stood there in the full gale of the North Atlantic and watched till the last light of home dipped into the sea.

NOVA SCOTIA

W*elcome to Nova Scotia. Lick-a-Chick.*
Those were the first two signs of Canadian life seen by this Newfoundlander rolling onto Cape Breton on the way to the mainland. I had heard rumours of this sign directing drivers to a chicken takeout and as Darrell and I drove bleary-eyed after a sleepless night bouncing on the gulf between Newfoundland and North America, I was strangely reassured by the Lick-a-Chick. Perhaps I felt more at ease knowing this journey was starting with something not completely unknown, albeit something truly bizarre.

The trip across the straits from Port aux Basques to North Sydney is often a rough rebirth for Newfoundlanders. The passage across the gulf is a labour they knew was coming and had been planning for, but had no idea could possibly be this hard once the final push finally came. And then the ferry doors open onto the new world and the light floods your eyes and you are pushed out into a strange new environment and you struggle to catch your breath in the air. The only thing missing is for some giant masked fella dressed all in white to lift you by the ankles and smack your arse.

From Port aux Basques to North Sydney is a rough eight-hour ferry ride at the best of times. And that's the short way. Darrell and I took the long way.

We took the ferry from Argentia to North Sydney, which can take anywhere from eighteen to twenty-four hours one way. There was not so much as a place to sit down by the time we rolled onto the boat, and it was a barf fest from start to finish with every other person hurling left, right, and centre.

I had lived in a university frat-like house with four to six others, on the road in one cheap hotel room with three others, eaten mostly chicken nuggets and fries off a cookie sheet from a toaster oven or day-old subs microwaved in a gas station until the plastic wrap gave way. I had slept in my gig clothes, and sink-washed underwear and socks as I went. I was hardly used to luxury or above-average travel and accommodations. I grew up in a fishing town and spent more than my share of time on boats of various sizes and in all kinds of weather. And still the ferry was the most awful experience of my life. It didn't matter to us that the cabins were all taken, as we couldn't afford one anyway. The seating areas looked like a shantytown, with people tenting off areas to lie on the floor. Couples and families worked in teams as one person draped a blanket over their claimed territory and another hunted for food and water. It was like a turf war for the first two hours. The remaining seventeen, no better.

I vowed there and then in the fall of 1993 to never do it again, if I could help it. As I type here this morning, nearly twenty-five years later, after thousands of trips abroad, I have yet to make a return trip on the ferry to or from Newfoundland. I have never recommended it to a single person visiting the place I love so well. Not one time.

The only thing more dodgy than that boat ride was our trip to get on it in the first place.

We'd done a Ford Festiva/Honda Civic hatchbacks week-end in Marystown at the legendary and infamous Circle A, housed in the Motel Mortier. The hotel, known around the band world as the Plywood Palace, featured just about everything an up-and-coming travelling act might want: a bar to play in and cheap rooms to stay in. I believe, in fact, the club gave us one room with two beds and two pull-out cots along with some kind of door deal where we got to keep most of what we made from the cover charge.

We'd decided a few weeks prior that for our first mainland run in Halifax we needed a car, so to save two flights and a rental fee, the Festiva or the Civic would make the trip with two bodies in it. I volunteered to be one of those, as I'd never done the boat trip. Darrell would be crashing with his girlfriend, who was at university in Halifax and had access to parking, so we decided we should take his car.

With the Circle A gig behind us, we said a few thank-yous and goodbyes to some of my cousins and aunts and uncles. My mother is from Marystown, and I was grateful to have some family in the audience. They certainly bolstered the crowd and would give me great chatting points during my next call home when Mom would inevitably ask, "Did you see anyone you knows?" At around two in the morning, Darrell and I were to make the two-and-a-half-hour drive up the Burin Peninsula and back east to Argentia to catch the ferry.

Darrell, affable as ever, walked over and shook hands with Uncle Sam. "Thanks so much for coming out. Grand to see a crowd."

My uncle Sam was happy to chat as well. "So Alan tells me you're making your way up the peninsula overnight to catch the early ferry. That's a bit of a dangerous drive with all the moose, but you should be all right on a clear night like tonight."

Darrell was grateful for the heads-up. "Thanks. Just got to gas up before we rolls and we should be golden."

My uncle's face lost its smile instantly. His eyebrows lifted up his long and wide forehead. "You don't have any gas?"

"We figured we'd gas up before we left. Where's the closest place?" Darrell said, holding a cigarette ready to light the moment he got outside.

Uncle Sam's eyebrows pushed further north on his forehead. "B'ys. Is two o'clock in the morning. There's not a gas station open anywhere on the Burin Peninsula until eight a.m. Do you have enough gas to make it the hundred kilometres back up to Goobies?"

"Not a chance." Darrell spun the cigarette in his hand, acknowledging we found ourselves in a pickle.

After a quick look, Darrell figured he had enough gas to get twenty-five kilometres max. It was a true townie mistake to assume you could get gas 24/7. We had the Civic loaded with everything the band had to its name, and seemingly no chance to ever get it or us where we needed to be.

"Frig sakes," I whinged. "We're kicking off our first-ever trip to the mainland in fine form by missing the friggin' ferry."

"Don't worry your Petty Harbour dog arse off yet," said Darrell, as upbeat and unfazed as ever. "There's more than one way to skin a cat."

As Darrell was no doubt recalling a shanty to sing, over his shoulder Uncle Sam had assembled a few people in a semicircle. As I approached I heard a few mumblings about chainsaws and lawn mowers, and by the time I fully arrived, a plan had been hatched to get us up the road to Goobies.

Uncle Sam spelled out the plan like a quarterback in a huddle. "All right. Joe here's got a half a can of unmixed gas for his saw, and Doug figures there's about five dollars' worth left in his lawn mower can, so we'll round that up, but that won't get you where you need to go, but Roger says his son just filled up his trike and only drove her up from the beach once with a load of nets, so there should be almost twenty dollars' worth in there, so we just got to siphon it out and he'll replace it in the morning when the station opens, now the only problem there is, the trike is locked in the shed and he got the keys gone to town, so we'll have to find a way to break in there but that should be no sweat, sure."

And with that seemingly dubious plan, three or four fellas nodded and dispersed with not only a confidence in their stride but a twinkle in their eye to get a chance to do something as foolish as rounding up gas cans, breaking into a shed, and stealing gas from a trike. What a nightcap to a concert at the Circle A.

Darrell and I drove his Civic on fumes over to somebody's shed. By the time we arrived, the first of the fellas to leave the huddle were already there with three half-filled gas cans ready to fill our tank. They had the cap off and the nozzle inserted with the red container held in the air before we could even get out of the car. A NASCAR pit crew could scarce have been so efficient.

Another gent had produced a multi-tool that somehow he already had with him and was on his knees in front of two barn-like shed doors. "Did he have that in his pocket at the concert?" I whispered to Darrell. A few others held their cigarette lighters near his face to help him see the screws in the lock casing. I had not yet made it to the shed when the b'ys behind me put the gas cap back on the car and shouted, "Got three cans in there," just before the fella on his knees stood and pulled open the shed doors, revealing a large Honda three-wheel all-terrain vehicle. One of the men behind me strode past with the now empty gas can and said, "Use this," as he produced a piece of garden hose about six feet long.

"Did he have *that* in his pocket at the concert?" Darrell whispered to me.

The kneeling fella was kneeling again, now next to the trike. He skilfully slid one end of the hose into the tank and the other into his mouth. One quick suck and gas ran from the ATV into the can on the ground beside him. He spit a little to get the taste of gas out of his mouth and reached into his jacket pocket, producing a plastic flask of Lamb's rum. He took a long swig before passing it around. "He *definitely* had that in his pocket at the concert!" Darrell and I said simultaneously.

In no time at all the boys were putting the gas cap back on the Civic and sending us on our way with the tank gauge reading just over half. Uncle Sam smiled a content smile as he closed the passenger door for me. "That'll get you to Goobies, for sure." We offered money, but they wouldn't take it. It was as if the joy of the chase was payment enough. "No worries, b'ys," Uncle Sam said. "Now get to the mainland and show them how it's done." The kneeler fella added, "And don't forget about us when ye are rock stars."

As if the journey across the island of Newfoundland and the straits was not long enough, upon arrival at the Lick-a-Chick sign, we still had to drive across Cape Breton Island and its linking causeway in the pitch-black darkness before getting to the actual mainland and eventually into Halifax, the most important city in the world.

Perhaps this is a good time for a bit of a geography lesson, as seen through the eyes of a band working out of St. John's.

More often than not, bands need easy, inexpensive access to urban centres to survive. The more cities you can reach from home, the cheaper it is to operate your band. It's as simple as that. Take a band from Toronto, Ontario. Let's assume that a five-hour trip is manageable for a young, eager band. They would depart home at ten in the morning, drive till mid-afternoon, set up and play a gig till eleven, and have everyone home by four.

Drop your pencil on Toronto and draw a five-hundred-kilometre circle around the city. Assume a "major urban centre" has around twenty-five thousand people or more. Count how many cities this size a band from Toronto can access. There would be dozens, at least, when you include Southern Ontario, Upstate New York, Ohio, and so on. Now draw the same circle around St. John's, Newfoundland. Count how many stops of the same size a band from home can reach in a day. Okay, I'll save you the trouble. The answer is none. Now double the distance to a thousand clicks and repeat the exercise for both cities. Count again for the Toronto band and there are now nearly hundreds of urban centres available to them. For the St. John's band, the answer is still none.

The harsh reality of being in a band based out of St. John's is undeniable. You have easy and inexpensive access to exactly no large or even medium urban audiences outside your home. Not one, in any direction. Even a band from the Northern Ontario town of Timmins, say, is in a much better position. Draw an eight-hour circle around Timmins, and the entire Golden Horseshoe of Southern Ontario falls within it. A Timmins band could drive for eight hours and pass by ten million people, I figure. The same band from St. John's could leave the city and drive for eight hours and pass fewer than forty thousand.

This geographical challenge never really hit home until Darrell and I were some twenty-five hours into a journey over road and sea and still had another four hours to go before finally reaching Halifax. All of which brings me to the point of just how important Halifax is to a touring band from Newfoundland. It's often seen as the end of the tour for most Canadian bands, perhaps a city you'd love to get to one day if the band's reach gets big enough, or if the crazy notion of going east of Quebec City strikes. But for Great Big Sea, Halifax was the most important city in the world. St. John's was home, but we needed a foothold on the mainland of Canada if we were to make any kind of living in the music business without moving to Toronto. And Halifax was it.

Nova Scotia is like a cousin to Newfoundland. Not a cousin who lives down the road, but one who lives in another province who you see every other summer. You are expected to know a lot about each other, but you really don't until you meet in university and spend some actual time together. I imagined when most mainlanders thought of Atlantic Canada they pictured Nova Scotia with its tidy, quaint fishing villages where happy lobster fishermen had names that started with Mac. I knew the province had a lot of universities and I often wondered why they had so many and Newfoundland had only one. I knew some famous musicians were from there. Anne Murray, John Allan Cameron, and I could have sworn Stan Rogers was from there too, though it turns out he was from Ontario and just spent many a summer in Nova Scotia, enough time though to inspire so many of his songs. My brother Bernie and I were massive hockey fans and knew that NHL stars Al MacInnis and Mike McPhee were from Nova Scotia. That is about all I knew about the place.

The first time Darrell and I travelled across Cape Breton in the dark, the sun rose just as we drove across the causeway that joins the island portion to the mainland. I was continually struck by how lush and green everything seemed. I had assumed because of the mining and fishing that Nova Scotia would be a rocky place with jagged cliffs heading down to the water, just like home. Not so. Not so at all. Turns out you can have farming and fishing right next to each other. Who knew? I daydreamed of what a meadow might look like close to the ocean in my rocky hometown, but found I could never quite picture it, and fell into passenger-seat sleep.

I was jolted awake as the car bumped onto the Macdonald Bridge, which seemed impossibly suspended between Dartmouth and Halifax, I gripped the seat belt and the door handle till my knuckles went white. I'd never been in a car on a road this high up in my life. I was about to shout the Lord's name in terror, but was calmed and fascinated by what lay beneath the bridge. What I saw out the window was much more of a city than I'd imagined. Halifax had many more tall buildings than St. John's, and the harbour itself seemed quite a bit busier than St. John's. The shipyard below me made the one in St. John's look tiny. There were long supply ships headed in and out of the basin, and what seemed like dozens of modern navy ships around a very active-looking navy base.

That morning, on the Macdonald Bridge, Darrell and I looked at each other after what had now been close to a thirty-hour journey, and unprompted, said to each other, "Fresh ground. Yes, b'y!" And we did a little happy dance in celebration.

After a few hours on Darrell's girlfriend's couch, my task was to find accommodations for the rest of the week. Darrell of course would be sorted. Séan had great friends in Halifax who had a spare room in their apartment and were more than happy to let him stay there as long as he wanted. So, with Séan and Darrell securing free accommodations for what would become the first of many week-long residencies in Halifax, we agreed that it was only fair that Bob and I find a free spot, or pay for our own place to sleep. Bob had flown to Ontario for a quick visit with his wife-to-be, and as we knew no one we could crash with, it was down to me to find us a room. I was pretty sure I knew, but I'd felt compelled to ask Bob for a brief description of what he might be after. "Any room within walking distance to the club with two beds and a door that closes," he responded as expected. "And as close to free as possible."

I'm sure there are readers wondering why an organized gang like ourselves would not have arranged all this well in advance. This was before the days of searching "low-priced accommodations for nocturnal folk musicians from Newfoundland" on your iPhone. I knew there was a Holiday Inn in Halifax and another hotel called the Lord Nelson, but I did not even bother to call their toll-free numbers, as we could not afford anywhere near their rates. I needed a cheap B & B or hotel in the downtown area. Darrell's girlfriend had gone through the phone book for us and found two or three suggestions. I was off on foot to find them.

One of the recommendations was a B & B on Hollis Street, near the waterfront. I walked down Robie until I hit Spring Garden, then turned downhill towards the harbour. A navy ship sailed through the bay followed closely by a large container ship, and I thought of Hugh MacLennan's *Barometer Rising*, a novel about the Halifax explosion of 1917, when a ship carrying explosives collided with another in this very harbour, flattening an entire neighbourhood not far from where I was walking. I had read MacLennan's novel in high school and been fascinated with the victims and heroes of that day and how many storylines must have wound together as the dust settled. This was the first time I'd visited a place I'd read about.

Wandering towards the B & B, past the well-kept old wooden warehouses in the Historic Properties, I could not help but wonder why we did not have more of this kind of thing in St. John's. We had an older harbour and a longer history of merchant trading than this city, yet Halifax seemed to have saved an entire block or so of waterside history that St. John's had not. I continued along the waterside trail skirting the harbour. It was so pleasant to walk along the edge of the ocean so near the heart of the downtown business district, and it remains one of my favourite city walks in the world.

Just up from the harbour walk was the Hollis Street B & B. I knocked on the door. The gent who seemed to be the owner noted that they were full and asked what kind of budget I had in mind. I repeated Bob's "as close to free as possible."

"Well"—he paused and took a breath—"there's an old place on Inglis Street that might still be renting rooms. I'm not sure, to be honest. Drop into the Hollis Hotel and get them to phone over for you. I think the same owner owns both places, but like I said, I'm not sure."

It wasn't much to go on, but it was enough for me. I dropped into the fancy Hollis Hotel and told them I was interested in a room at another place I'd heard they managed that might be closer to my budget. The lady behind the desk somewhat reluctantly gave me directions and said she'd call ahead for me.

The hundred-year-old Inglis House stood three storeys high on a narrow but deep lot on Inglis Street in downtown Halifax, not far from St. Mary's University. What was so haunting about the place was not how rundown it was, but how beautiful it so clearly had been. Behind a short front garden that may once have been considered formal rested a couple of decorative iron chairs and small round tables that looked like they might have been used for high tea, but not since World War Two. White paint peeled off the seats of the chairs and the top of the tables, exposing the rusty age underneath. Each was missing at least one leg, but somehow still stood. The same could be said for the house itself.

I imagined this place had been grand in its day, which was well over a hundred thousand days ago, I figured. Now, blue and white paint fell from the siding and trim, which was dotted with holes in the rotting wood. I remembered my days on the wharf in Petty Harbour, wondering if a rat could fit through the holes in the fish plant walls. Here, I wondered if a cat would fit through the holes as big as my fist. I walked up the broken, tilted concrete walkway and could not help but notice the enormous wood-framed windows on the main floor.

At least six feet high, they were surrounded by intricate carvings that must have once been spectacular but had fallen into disrepair, leaving the figures mutilated and harrowing. A bird with no beak. An elf with no hat. A rabbit with half an ear. And more disturbing, a naked and very obviously male child, its face screaming in pain. Most disturbing was that its face was not where it should have been. There was just a jagged surface at the front its skull. Its face lay in its upturned hands.

I turned my gaze upward to the top-floor windows framed under triangular dormers and noticed the not-so-white-anymore lace curtain was pulled back just enough to let a girl see out.

She stood bent at the waist, one hand on the yellowing lace, the other shading her eyes and pressed to the glass. I guessed her to be in her mid-twenties, but her face was somewhat obscured by her hand, so I could not say for sure. The moment our eyes met, she retreated and let the curtain fall back to cover the window. Her spying made me a little uncomfortable, but I had few choices, and did not break stride.

I went up the creaky wooden steps to the door with cracked stained glass sidelights, and turned the little knob in the door that struck a bell as it rotated. I heard the steps of more than one pair of feet scurrying up and down the stairs. Two people were shouting and whispering and giggling in what I assumed was an argument over who would open the door.

I finally heard someone coming closer to the front door. As it swung open, I was afforded a clear view down a long hallway with what must have been twenty-foot ceilings and a chandelier with only a few working bulbs. The hallway was lined with portraits of men in suits and formal hunting clothes. At the end of the hall, a half door into what seemed to be a kitchen served as a sort of check-in counter. The light from the windows behind it blinded me, and I thought I saw a shadow of a person scuttle across it. As my eyes adjusted and I stepped fully into the hall, the person who'd let me in finally spoke, closing the door behind me. Her voice was low and quiet, and she greeted me as if I were entering a funeral home and had asked directions to the proper corpse.

"Straight ahead to check-in to check in." I turned to see a woman in her twenties, but whose dress and hairdo suggested a much older person. "You must be Alan, the musician." The dust caught in my throat, so I nodded instead of answering out loud.

"They called us from the Hollis and said you might need a room for the week."

I coughed a couple of times. "Yeah." All I could manage was a whisper. "Me and Bob from the band need a room while we play the Lower Deck this week."

I heard a giggle from the reception kitchen, and saw the girl from the upstairs window lurking in the back.

"That's my sister, Rhonda. She helps here sometimes ... well, all the time."

"Oh, cool." I walked towards the half door. "And what's your name?"

Now an even bigger giggle from Rhonda.

"You shut up!" my guide shouted and then politely turned back to me. "I'm Marilyn. Welcome to the Inglis House. Let me get some keys and show you what we have available."

Marilyn grabbed her sister by the arm and they both disappeared down a back hallway to an office of some sort. I could hear them giggling and teasing each other in the distance.

I wandered back towards the front door, taking a closer look at what I was getting Bob and myself into. To the right, light beamed through the large windows into a room with high bookshelves, loaded with dusty novels and textbooks and volumes of *Encyclopaedia Britannica*. I pushed past the large wingback chairs, all in need of reupholstering, and stared at a painting of a ship in a storm. Waves beat in over the bow as men jumped for their lives. A giant tentacle pointed high out of the sea, and whatever monster it belonged to was about to smash the ship to splinters. The fireplace below the painting had been stuffed full of insulation and covered with a near-transparent plastic Sobeys shopping bag, stretched and taped to the edges.

I tried to read some of the spines on the shelves. I gave a quick blow and a mini cloud of dust puffed up in my face. I squinted as I waited for it to settle. I could make out some classics, *The Old Man and the Sea* and *Shane* and a bunch of westerns by Louis L'Amour. On the other side of the fireplace the bookshelves held a number of trophies and small statues. I bent down to read the inscriptions—and came face to face with a large rat up on its back legs, baring its teeth at me.

"Jesus!" I jumped back and bumped into a chair, but the rat did not move a muscle. It glared at me with an unblinking eye. It was perfectly still. Eerily still. Impossibly still. And it was a mink, not a rat. I laid my hand on the wingback chair and pushed myself up to my feet. Almost. A voice from somewhere nearly sent me to my grave.

"Not the same when they're stuffed, are they?"

"Jesus Christ!" I fell back into the shelves, causing the mink to fall against my butt. I could feel its teeth against my jeans. I reached behind and yanked it off as if it was eating me, then, quickly feigning cool and calm, I placed the mink back on its shelf.

There in one of the large chairs sat a man of some considerable age. At first glance, he gave the appearance of a retired university professor who had not changed his clothes since his last class sometime around the end of World War Two. His tattered dark blue blazer with holes in the patches on the elbows suggested someone not quite ready to admit he's wearing rags. He slicked his dirty grey hair over his balding head and smiled, revealing teeth in need of a dentist's attention.

"I do some of the taxidermy myself," he said in a voice as deep and resonant as thunder. "I like the permanence of it. Often wish there was an equivalent for us humans, don't you?" He had a tinge of an English accent that may have been put on.

I was still having a heart attack so could not muster an answer.

"Just checking in to Inglis House? I hear the girls frittering about. Forgive them. We don't get many guests here."

"Oh. Yeah." I was gathering myself and steadying the mink back on its hind legs. "Do you work or stay here?" I asked.

"Me? Yes. Something like that." The old man turned his gaze back to the plastic Sobeys bag where there once would have been a roaring fire.

A cold silence hung in the air until Marilyn called out from the half door. "Here, Alan, I'll show you the room." We walked back down the hall past the portraits, and I swore I felt the eyes of the men in suits following me.

As she led me up a creaky and shaky but beautiful staircase, I asked her who the gent in the chair was.

"Oh, he's no one," was all she said.

I never saw that man again or ever learned who he might be, but not once in hundreds of early and late and sober and not at all sober occasions did I enter that house without checking to see if he was back.

At the top of the stairs was a large landing with four doors. The hardwood floor was worn and in need of a polish, but the boards ran so perfectly parallel to the wall you could see they had been laid by expert hands. Marilyn led me to one of the doors, and unlocking it with a key from the *Titanic*, she pointed to the next door and said, "There's the bathroom. You share it with the others."

The door opened onto a room with an amazing chandelier in its centre; another amazing chandelier with only a few working bulbs. Paint peeled off the plaster walls. Empty hooks hung on bare walls. A single enormous window would have let a ton of light in if it or the lace curtain on it had been at all clean.

"That don't open," she said. I looked from the window to the fireplace. "That don't work," she said.

The room had two twin beds sitting about ten inches from each other. And that was all. There was no phone, chairs or desk, end tables, lamps or closets.

A room with two beds. Marilyn was not lying.

"It's perfect," I said.

"Like they told you at the Hollis, it's usually $30 per night, but if you rent for the week it's only $175. And you have to pay up front. There's a pay phone downstairs. It only works sometimes, but if you want to use our phone, me or Rhonda probably won't mind."

I handed her $175 cash and she gave me two keys, each on a metal key tag with *INGLIS HOUSE* engraved in block letters. She closed the door behind her as she left. Marilyn and the mystery professor were the first two mainlanders I ever really spoke to on my first professional trip to Canada. "Well, now," I said to myself. "Perhaps all the peculiar ones are not in Newfoundland after all."

And so I checked in to a room that would become my home away from home for much of the next year. The host girls would get so familiar with our schedules that they would screen our calls. Our girlfriends would phone from home to hear another girl's voice answer, "Inglis House," and when they asked to speak with us they would be told they could not, as "Alan is still sleeping. They were out very late last night, and I don't think he even had his usual sub sandwich with him when he came back, so he is probably really hungry, too. And Rhonda said he is out of toothpaste, but don't worry about that, because we got lots of toothpastes here. Please call back later."

The strangest thing about our time in the Inglis House is that, over hundreds of nights, I did not see a single other guest come or go.

If Halifax is holy ground for Newfoundland bands, then the Lower Deck was our cathedral. On a rainy Monday in the fall of 1993, Darrell and Séan rounded up Bob and me from Inglis House. We unloaded our stuff onto a downtown street and walked it across a cobblestone footpath and down the steps under the Lower Deck's awning. There, taped on the square glass window of the old wooden door, was a photocopied 8½-by-11 poster with a grainy picture of our four faces and stylized letters around our grins. *From Newfoundland! Great Big Sea.* It was the first time I'd ever seen us billed as "From Newfoundland."

We had not asked them to put this on the sign. Yet there it was. The first thing. As big as the band name. It gave me great comfort for reasons I could not yet fully understand.

This club had been described to me in some detail, so I knew what to expect: a small cellar-like room with a low ceiling. But I was struck as I entered by just how small it was and just how low the ceiling was. The floors and wall were stone, and beautifully restored wooden beams spanned the ceiling. A taller person would have to duck. Long, narrow wooden tables with matching benches filled the place from the windows down one side to the bar on the other. There was barely enough space to lay down our gear.

"Can they really jam a hundred plus people in here?" I asked.

"Yep," Bob muttered. "Cheek by jowl."

The owner, Greg, was waiting to show us around. It didn't take long. We walked along the short rear side of the rectangular room that, the more I surveyed it, did bear a striking resemblance to the lower deck of a ship. A narrow walkway made a perimeter for patrons and servers to get around the tables and up to the bar. "Not much room for anything but singing and drinking," I said. "Songs and beers. What else is there?"

I could not help but notice how clean the place was. The spotless floors, the polished bar, the dented and scratched but sparkling wooden tables, and nothing but the delightful smell of fresh sea air coming in through the open windows. I let my hand glide along the polished bar and noticed a few traditional pub taps but also a high-tech-looking computerized draft beer delivery system. Greg must have caught me eyeing it with some wonder.

"One click and the tap delivers an eight-ounce glass of ice-cold beer in about three seconds," he told us. "The larger one is for pitchers. If you fellas do as well as I think you will, we'll have a tap suck party some night."

I would have asked what a tap suck party was, but I really wanted to get to the little stage, which was on the smaller side but manageable even with its very low ceiling height. "No jumping here, b'ys, unless you can do it sideways," I was sizing up the tidy PA with its mixing desk tucked inside an old fireplace and multiple speakers hidden in the beams above our heads. No need to push a rack and speakers over the cobblestones here. This place was wired and ready.

Sound check done. Three hours until our first-ever gig on the mainland, and I needed to rid myself of anxious energy. I wandered the streets in the rain. I sought refuge in a coffee shop on the bottom of Spring Garden Road.

The twenty-something fella behind the counter welcomed me. "Some rainy. Friggin' spillin', b'y."

I instantly recognized a Newfoundland accent, but I could not tell where from exactly.

"Hey, yeah. Pouring." I was glad to be in out of it.

"You're that buddy, right?" His accent was getting thicker.

"Sorry?" I asked.

He pointed to a photocopied page on the wall just like the one on the window at the Lower Deck. "You're buddy from town playin' at the Deck this week. All the Newfs are comin' down."

"Oh yeah. I'm Alan." I extended my hand like a real townie and he shook it, though I could tell he thought it not necessary. A non-townie. "You from home?" A question I asked for the first time, and one I've asked a thousand times since.

"Yeah, Deer Lake. Up doin' phys ed degree at Dal. Bunch of us heard a band from home were comin' to the Deck so we're gettin' on 'er and comin' down Thursday."

"Oh, cool. Thanks."

"Dyin' for a bit of accordion, b'y. All they minds is fiddles up here. Hardly any singin' at all. Just tunes after tunes. Drive ya cracked."

"Oh yeah?"

"Yes, b'y. My cousin from town says he see ye all the time on George Street. Says ye does a pile of old songs from home in a new way. Can't wait."

"Yeah, first night tonight. Just got off the ferry yesterday. A bit tired but looking forward to it."

"I never been to the Lower Deck, to tell ye the truth, but dyin' to show this crowd what a proper night out is like. Bringin' a gang from the volleyball team, so it could be rowdy. Hopefully the girls' team will follow us or ye'll be lookin' at a pile of drunk dudes all night."

We were all about an hour early for the show and hung around back by the kitchen. I could not take the nervousness of pacing back there and decided to do a lap of the club and get a sense of what it might be like. To my surprise, the place was already about half-full. Turns out, the Lower Deck attracts folks from all over the country. The university students, the travelling business people, the navy gang, and the tourists all added up to a diverse sampling of people from across Canada. There were Nova Scotians in the audience for sure, but there were many others from many other parts of the country too.

As ever, Darrell had a few buddies who recognized me and asked for a few Newfoundland tunes. I assured them we had that in spades. A group of businessmen who were on a conference at the hotel next door said they were looking for some "Atlantic Canadian" music. I wasn't sure I knew for sure what that meant and it must have showed on my face, as one of them specified, "You know, 'Farewell to Nova Scotia' and 'Barrett's Privateers,' right?"

"Of course!" I said with certainty, and then wondered why I did. I had sung "Barrett's Privateers" as a solo dude a year or so previous, but had no memory of Great Big Sea doing it. As for "Farewell to Nova Scotia," I could mime the chorus but had only the most passing knowledge of the song's verses.

Now ten minutes till show time, I walked straight back to the kitchen area and casually mentioned to the boys that I'd promised we'd sing these two songs.

"No sweat!" Darrell said, upbeat as ever.

"Cool. You know them?"

"I'm sure between us we can do 'Barrett's.'" Darrell was half in and half out of the door with a smoke held out in the rain, and I asked if we could do "Farewell to Nova Scotia" as well.

"For sure!"

"Cool! You know the words?"

"No, Jesus, no."

And with that, we went onstage.

The crowd wanted to sing, and we wanted them to sing with us. The Newfoundland contingent nearly stood in reverence when we played "I's the B'y" and "Rant and Roar." And they nearly took the roof off the place when we played "Lukey's Boat."

For the entire first set I avoided eye contact with the fella who'd asked for "Farewell to Nova Scotia," but by the second set I could avoid it no longer. "A special request for 'Farewell to Nova Scotia'!" I shouted. "Please, please help us sing along!" I launched into the starting chorus and got the audience singing. By the inevitable first verse, I'd spotted a couple singing away in the corner and implored them, "You guys lead us in the verses!" They were only too happy to oblige. Somehow we faked our way through a beloved song that none of us really knew. And got tremendous applause for it.

On that rainy Monday night, one thing was becoming clear. If we were the wrong band for the 401 club in Stephenville, we were the right band for the Lower Deck in Halifax. Students, sailors, travelling businesspeople, and tourists, they all came to drink beer and sing along with Atlantic Canadian music. Songs from Newfoundland were just as welcome as Nova Scotia songs, and even Irish songs that Atlantic Canadians might have sung regularly or found influential in the local tradition.

I chatted with the doorman after that first gig. Mark was a big fella to say the least, and I could tell he'd been around the club a while, as he seemed to have the respect of everyone in the place, including Greg the owner.

After the crowd had left, he offered me a beer and a stool, and I was glad to take both. "You're off to a grand start here." He clinked his glass with mine. "I'm on this door a lot. Seen a lot of bands. You guys have something special. Won't be long before you're too big for this place. I gotta tell you this, though. Six or seven nights in a row here can be hard on the liver. I seen more than one good band blow a wicked run because the nights out got the better of them. No trouble to be good on Monday on night one. Let's make sure you're just as good, or better, on night six. Mind the free beer here and the foolishness as you wander up the hill after the shows. It's been the undoing of manys a good fella."

He tipped his glass, inhaled the rest of his beer, zipped up his jacket, and slapped my back. "See you tomorrow night."

The heart and soul of those early visits to Nova Scotia was always to be found at the Lower Deck. When I cast my memory back, it feels like we walked on that stage only once, and got off it about a year later. We played a week-long run once or twice a month for that entire winter and into the summer with crowds growing to capacity six and seven nights a week. Regional concert promoters and label representatives came to see the band, but I couldn't tell you if they came on a Tuesday in October or a Friday in February.

Before too long we were being courted by major record labels and national booking companies. And then we landed a gig at the biggest festival back home in Newfoundland. The Salmon Festival was held in Grand Falls, in the central part of the island, and often attracted thousands if not tens of thousands of people. We were to be one of a few acts opening for our heroes, the Rankin Family. So in the summer of 1994, we rolled into the Lower Deck to play our last run of nights there. The final night of the run was July 15, and it was a ripper. If memory serves, we played one set, took a short break, and then played for almost two hours until closing.

Mark, still on the door, was unusually quiet that night and was a little emotional when we chatted after. "Well, I said you weren't long for this place, didn't I? Come on, then, hug it out, before you gets too famous to remember the likes of me."

After learning far too well what a tap suck party was (my head still hurts when I think of it), we bid farewell to the Lower Deck and a "see you soon" to Nova Scotia. As the plane took off, I looked out the window over Halifax and felt a warm familiarity with the harbour and the streets. How wonderful to have had a home away from home in Halifax. I cannot think of a better spot.

I could not help but hear a voice from my young life, the voice of my parents' parents' generation when they cursed the day Newfoundland joined Canada. "They picked the right day to sign that declaration, April first. 'Cause they were all a bunch of fools to join up with the Canadian Wolf. Well, I did not suck the wolf's tit and I'm not going to start today or any day. I am a Newfoundlander like my father and his father before that."

I was eager to report to Mom that the place was lovely and the people kind. I was nervous about reporting to folks of my grandfather's age that there was not a single Canadian Wolf to be seen, as far as I could tell.

The plane pushed over the straits between Nova Scotia and Newfoundland, which seemed to pass in a blink on a Dash 8. "A lot quicker than the ferry!" I said to Darrell, then turned to see that he was sound asleep.

And rightly so. We were headed for the biggest gig of our lives.

We were headed home.

THE PURPLE DINOSAUR

After an early flight from Halifax to Gander, we doubled back to Grand Falls and rolled backstage at the mighty Salmon Festival. This festival was really getting going in the mid-nineties, and by the time we arrived in the early afternoon, several thousand people were pushed up to the front of the stage.

And what a stage it was. Huge speakers were stacked more than a storey high, and others were suspended from the rafters and scaffolding. Moving lights wheeled and spun, and fog machines flooded the stage with a creeping mist that made the performers look like they were angels floating on a cloud as they sang and played.

A gent who identified himself as Gerry led us backstage, which was really more like a compound created by the wire fences of the park and the long rows of mobile office trailers and RVs serving as production offices, catering trucks, and dressing rooms. I followed our guide as we made our way down the line of trailer doors, and there amid the Rankin Family and other acts, all bands we respected, some we even idolized, was a simple off-white dressing-trailer door with simple black lettering on a white sign that read, *GREAT BIG SEA*.

Inside was a black leather couch, two matching chairs, a floor lamp, mirror, and a coffee table with water, soft drinks, and beer. Free beer. "Holy mother of shite!" was all I could think, and "We made it, b'ys. We made it," was all I could say.

Gerry asked if we needed anything else. I looked at the water, Cokes, and beer and honestly thought, "What else could anyone possibly need?"

After about an hour of nervous energy and arguing about the set list, we hit the stage. By this point there were close to ten thousand people in the audience, by far the biggest crowd we'd ever played to. Most of the other bands had drums and keyboards and amplifiers and sound technicians, but of course we had none of that. Just Darrell and his bass, me with an acoustic guitar, Séan with his bodhran, and Bob with an accordion or mandolin or tin whistle or fiddle.

"Who's ready for the greatest kitchen party in Newfoundland history!" Answering my call, shouts and cheers rang around the field. People jumped from their lawn chairs to sing and dance with us before we'd played a single chord.

We ripped into our set as if we owned the place, and a few tunes later, we did. We spent the next few hours watching the other bands from the wings because we could, and basked in what was easily the triumph of our short career so far.

As the Rankins were blowing the place away with their modernized Cape Breton folk music and brother Jimmy's original songs, I nipped away to grab a drink from our trailer. I cast my eyes around the room like it was the Taj Mahal, and there amongst the paraphernalia was what appeared to be a Salmon Festival programme. I figured I would skim through it to see our photo and bio, as I assumed that was the kind of thing newly crowned rock stars did. I flipped to the middle and the schedule of events. I opened another of the free beer and sipped it as my eyes went right to our name on the Saturday schedule, there amongst the names of my heroes. I thought I'd have a look at the Sunday stuff to see if there might be someone cool to watch.

The daytime section featured a large photo of what looked like Barney the dinosaur, who'd be doing a kids' show at 11 a.m. There was a brief description of Barney's biggest hits, like "I Love You, You Love Me," and right underneath the bio, in the tiniest print, it read, "Opening set by Great Big Sea."

I was puzzled. I had heard nothing about playing an opening set on Sunday. I had been celebrating like we had the next evening off, and most certainly the next morning off! I figured this must be a mistake, as no one in our camp had ever heard of this 8:30 a.m. set-up and 9:30 a.m. start. I made my way back to the stage area, and over the next hour or so tried to get the attention of one of my bandmates who could confirm or deny the commitment the next morning, but the Rankins were still going, so it was midnight before I could ask anyone about the schedule. The guys shook their heads and shrugged. None of them had ever heard of this early matinee opening set. For Barney the dinosaur.

We finally tracked down Gerry, who had been celebrating the evening as much as we had. "Hey, Gerry, I noticed a line in the schedule about us opening for Barney in the morning?"

"Yes, thanks so much for doing it, b'ys. The kids are really gonna love it. Hope ye does that 'What Are You At' song. My grandson loves it." And with that he turned away and disappeared into a circle of people in varying states of disrepair.

We all looked at each other, resigned to the fact that our rock and roll evening was about to be curbed by the fact that we had to be back here in about seven hours in the cold, hard light of morning to open for some dude in a purple dinosaur suit.

It was after one thirty when we got back to the hotel, and the lobby bar was on wheels. Jimmy and some of the Rankin sisters waved us into the pub. It would have been rude to not respond.

It was well after three when I finally pressed my head to the pillow.

The alarm clock went off at 7:30, and I raced to the shower. It was ice cold, which may or may not have helped. At eight an awaiting minivan ferried us back to the site.

The huge suspended speakers were gone, replaced with much smaller ones left lying on the massive empty stage. The moving lights were gone, replaced by nothing but harsh daylight. The fog machine was replaced by actual fog. Without the ten thousand concertgoers, the field just looked like a big empty soccer pitch. Garbage cans were tipped over, and torn bunting was strewn about the lonely venue. Just four lonely mics on four tiny stands tipping in the wind.

Backstage, the trailers were empty. No couches with no matching chairs. There were no names on doors. We threw our stuff onstage and did a terrible sound check as moms and dads and Barney fans, bundled up to keep the rain off them, made their way to the front of the stage. They had no trouble, as by the time our set was to start, there may have been four hundred people in a field big enough for twenty thousand.

From the stage, all I could see through the mist were dozens of young Barney fans fully and completely disappointed they'd have to sit through someone who clearly was not Barney before getting to see the purple star they'd come for.

I walked to the mic to introduce the band and the show. I could think of nothing new to say that might engage the people in front of me so I impulsively resorted to the previous day's battle cry. "Who's ready for the greatest kitchen party in Newfoundland history!" But on this cold, wet morning there were no shouts and cheers. No one leapt to their feet, I guarantee you that. All I got back were looks of confusion from annoyed parents and mildly threatened children. The looks I got from the other members of the band were not much better. I was flustered, so I just let something come out of my mouth. Like a reflex. A jerking knee under a hammer. I shouted, "Hey, is anyone here hungover? Yeah, right? Wicked time last night! Come on, let's do it all again!" On the ground in front of me, moms pulled their frightened children closer.

We fumbled our way through a short set, and as the last chord lingered in the mist, there was barely the sound of a single pair of hands clapping to drown out the ground hum from the speakers.

Humiliated, I wandered back to the trailers, trying to figure a way to blame this defeat on someone else.

And then I saw him. A man, or I should say the neck and head of a man, poking out of a round, purple costume with oversized dinosaur feet and hands. He had a rounded belly and a long, thick, rigid tail that was lined with shark-like fins. On the trailer step next to him sat a purple head with wide-open eyes and a wider, even more open mouth frozen in mid-yelp. A most unfortunately happy creature decapitated mid-laugh.

"Well done up there, man," he said with a bright smile. "The kids can make for a tough crowd. You did better than most in the pre-dinosaur slot. They come for the big purple fella and have a hard time waiting for him. Don't let it get you down."

I wondered how much trouble I would get in for telling Barney to go f—k himself. Bad karma, I figured. So I thanked him instead. "Not our best, I'm afraid. Wrong time of day."

"You'll get them next time, man. Not to worry."

Then I wondered how much trouble I would get in for punching Barney right in the face. How would that look on the résumé?

I closed the trailer door behind me and looked around the old wood-panelled walls with leak marks and rot in the corners. Through the fog I could hear a few hundred fans calling for Barney.

That purple dinosaur rocked the place, by the way. And to this day, I swear by two things.

One: There is no gig in the world harder than opening for Barney on a wet Sunday morning.

And two: For every pat on the back, there's ten boots in the arse.

PRINCE EDWARD ISLAND

I stood in front of the hotel a short walk from the heart of downtown Charlottetown, Prince Edward Island. The green-and-white glowing sign beamed the name of the place: *Inn on the Hill*. I was confused by this. Growing up on the rocky cliffs of Newfoundland under the knolls surrounding Petty Harbour, I knew hills very well. I knew big hills, small hills, steep hills, tree-covered hills, and barren windswept hills. I had thrown rocks from hills into the ocean, and slid down snow-covered hills on an old garbage bag. I had walked up a hill to school, and somehow walked up another one on the way home. When bothering my mother with questions and foolishness, I was regularly told to "go run up and down a hill."

So standing here my first-ever day on P.E.I., in the parking lot of a hotel on an almost imperceptible bump in the road, I wondered: Where was the hill that this inn was meant to be on? Water would barely run down from this parking lot to the main road. We'd played street hockey on a piece of ground with more of a rise in it than this place.

Bob was always the smartest one, so I asked him. "Is this a hill?"

"It is in P.E.I., I suppose."

I knew only a few things about P.E.I. before I stood upon it. From Stompin' Tom's classic song "Bud the Spud" I knew to look for red soil and potatoes. I knew from the CBC that Anne of Green Gables was a famous person from the island and the subject of great literature, plays, musicals, television series, and feature films. Though to be perfectly honest, I'd not read, heard, or seen any of these things. I just knew she was a big deal over here. You can imagine my surprise when I learned shortly after arriving that she was an entirely fictional character. Honestly, I knew there were novels inspired by her life, but I always assumed, for good reason given all the fuss I might add, that she was at least at one time a flesh-and-blood human.

I also knew that P.E.I. had a serious lobster trade. My source for this information was primarily older fishermen in Petty Harbour, who frequently reminded themselves and anyone who would listen that our Newfoundland lobsters were, as Vincy once described them, "every bit as good as the ones they makes top dollar for up in P.E.I. Friggin' mainlanders gets everything, see."

One day, I felt bold. "But P.E.I. is an island like us and not really on the mainland."

"Yeah, well," Vincy shot back and pointed into the harbour, "you're not gonna be dry on the wharf like me in a minute if you don't close your trap."

And that's about all I could have told you about Prince Edward Island before our rented station wagon rolled off the ferry we'd taken that morning from Pictou County, Nova Scotia, to Wood Islands, P.E.I. But as soon as we arrived I was struck by how much this place looked exactly like it did on tourism postcards. You could see the famous red clay shores and beaches leading up to perfect grassy fields rolling gently to a barn or a farmhouse in the distance.

P.E.I. looked lush. It looked rich. To a fella from a place literally as hard as rocks, this place looked easy. The ground appeared more like Nestlé's Quik than soil. Like you could just add hot water and a drop of milk and drink it down. The soil seemed like it might sprout a root vegetable at any second. "Jesus," I said to the boys, "you could pick up a handful of sand and a potato would be growing there by the time you got to the store." I had never seen anything like it in eastern Newfoundland, and certainly not on the jagged bone-rock cliffs of Petty Harbour. I'd venture to say there was more fertile soil on one small farm than there was in my entire hometown.

"I cannot see a single rock, of any size, anywhere," I said to the gang. "What do they throw at each other when they gets pissed off?"

"Baymen," one of them answered.

As we made our way across the island, I couldn't help but notice how ordered and organized this place was, with its long, perfectly parallel rows dug into the soil. My harbour town seemed desperately random in comparison, with settlers' houses dropped higgledy-piggledy on the steep, hard hills, wherever seemed most impossible. As we drove down the perfect country road past well-kept farm after well-kept farm, each with a tidy mailbox on a stand with a little curved hook at the bottom for the newspaper, I tried my best to think of a roadway between the snaky hill paths of Petty Harbour and the zigzagging maze of old St. John's that was in any way as neat and easy to travel. I could not think of a single one.

Was it possible that the folks of my youth who trumpeted on about everything in my hometown being just about perfect and far better than anywhere else were mistaken? Jaysus, I wondered, had we Newfoundlanders been suffering from some national delusion? Was our heartfelt contentment with our own tough way of life a sign not of a people willing to make the most out of whatever cards they were dealt, but rather of simple stubbornness? Or a bit of both, perhaps?

Then, about halfway between the ferry dock and Charlottetown, we stopped at a small family-run gas station. While the attendant filled our tank, I got out of the car. I wanted to put my feet on the ground. I don't feel like I've been to a place until I step out of a car, plane, train, or boat and feel my feet on the closest thing to native soil. And I could see that P.E.I. had some serious soil, so I wanted to stand on it and feel the warmth of the glowing sun on my face, the same sun that fuelled the vegetable hampers of the nation.

It was like standing on a pile of flour. Gentle and soft underfoot. I wondered if I would sink right into it if I stood in the same place long enough. Not a single bit like Skinner's Hill in Petty Harbour. You could stand in one spot there for a thousand lifetimes and never feel the ground beneath you give a millimetre. Petty Harbour was a grindstone; P.E.I., a pillow.

In less than an hour, I saw signs for Charlottetown. Could this be right? Had we travelled a third of the way across the province already? I thought back to my childhood map, the little bit in the bay next to Halifax with only enough room for PIE.

Charlottetown was cleaner and better organized than any city I'd ever seen before. It was tough not to compare it with St. John's, not because it was so similar, but because I assumed it would be. Charlottetown appeared so well planned, with all its streets running at perfect right angles, whereas the streets of St. John's were born out of the harbour and drunkenly crawled up the surrounding hills every which way with no apparent logic. I've heard the streets of St. John's called "cow paths" more than once. Negotiating Charlottetown's grid-like map was no trouble at all. Following driving directions in St. John's is harrowing and confusing, and made all the more challenging by the fact that locals don't see what could possibly be easier.

Here's a comparison of two typical responses to a tourist asking how to get from the historic downtown's Water Street to the university campus in both Charlottetown and St. John's, in each case a distance of just a few kilometres as the crow flies.

Visitor: Excuse me, I need to drive from downtown to the university. What's the best route?

Charlottetown answer: Turn right on Queen Street and right on Belvedere Avenue. You should see the university right in front of you.

St. John's answer: No trouble at all. Nothing to it. Just go down Water towards Cabot Tower, but not all the way there, mind you. If you hits the water, you're gone too far. Turn up Prescott Street away from the water, and for Jesus' sakes don't stall or slip back in neutral or you'll be drowned for sure. Not that that happens more than a few times a year . . . in the summer. If it's icy in the winter, you see cars sliding all over the place but I wouldn't worry about that too much today. At the top of Prescott, you'll find yourself at what seems to be a dead end, but it's not. Turn right and enter Rawlins Cross. Some people calls that the most confusing intersection on the planet, but it's not so bad once you go through it . . . a few dozen times a week . . . for a few years. Trouble is, see, that intersection is really three or four intersections but it's all called the one thing for some reason. Turn right when you gets to a place where it looks like you can't, but right is really the only way you can go, though it looks like you've got eight or ten options. When that right-hand scoot-kind-of-thing takes you around where the old brown houses used to be, you wants to find the middle lane, which is nowhere near the middle, but that's what everyone calls it because it used to be in the middle before they expanded the intersection years ago. The middle lane is the one on the right-hand side of the middle part, not the far right-hand side, because that will just take you down by the Newfoundland Hotel and right back here where we are now. So just stay in the middle lane and head through the intersection. Now, right away when you gets through the lights, that road splits in three. Don't take the left one because you'll be right back in the intersection and back right here where we are now. You can take the right one if you like, but you might end up down past the park near the stadium by the lake on the one-way street up by the penitentiary and onto Forest Road and right back here where we are now. So probably best to take the middle lane, which, obviously, is the one on the left side. You should be on Monkstown Road then, which will carry you down to Empire Avenue. Now, you're not supposed to turn left on Empire, but everyone does it, because we always used to go that way till they decided it was too dangerous or something. So turn left unless you see the constabulary. Go along on Empire till you're just past Complete Rent-Alls and then turn almost right, not completely right, because the two roads there really comes together there more than intersecting, really. It's not like they're very square or anything. Head down that road towards the curling club, but if you gets to the curling club, you're gone too far. So just before the curling club, turn right up Bonaventure Avenue, which does turn into Allandale Road, but no one really knows where, and when you gets to the lights, before the Arts and Culture Centre, look to the left. Some of them buildings there are part of the university. Not all of them, mind you. But you should be pretty close to what you're looking for. Unless you wants the medical building over in the Health Sciences Centre, because that's another thing altogether.

Here in downtown Charlottetown, I could not find a single cow path or mysterious intersection. All 'round me, streets ran in a grid, except for the ones that neatly wrapped around the theatre and grounds built to memorialize the very place where the Confederation documents of Canada were signed.

Speaking of which, I saw Government of Canada signs everywhere. Every other building or corner or park seemed to be funded by Ottawa in some way or another. In my hometown of Petty Harbour, there was one Government of Canada sign, down by the single piece of wharf that almost no one used. There was slightly more federal presence in St. John's, but nothing like downtown Charlottetown. This city, not half the size of St. John's, appeared to have considerably more federal money poured into it, which, no doubt, helped make it a beautiful place.

So after a few hours in P.E.I., a sober thought entered my mind. What if my own ancestors crossing the ocean from the south of Ireland had known there was another island, just a few days' journey away past Newfoundland? One that boasted plenty of fish, where growing things in the ground was not akin to an episode of *Survivor*. What if they knew the capital city of this island would be well organized and have an amicable relationship with the federal government as opposed to being constantly at odds with it? And that this relationship would result in an obvious presence and support for the city, making it much more beautiful and economically successful? It occurred to me really for the first time that maybe, on paper, compared to some other close-by options, Newfoundland might not necessarily have been the most sensible choice for settlement. But, then again, we were not well known for being sensible, I supposed.

Later, I chatted with a wise friend of mine about how troubled I was to be doubting the assertion of my youth that Newfoundland is the greatest place on earth. This learned gent is as loyal a Newfoundlander as me, but was well into a rant, and even further into a bottle of whisky, as he posed this question back to me and the others in the pub: "Why the f—k did my ancestors stop where they did? Fools jumped ship two days too quick and ran like rats up the rocky beach to the first piece of land they saw since leaving Ireland. What godforsaken circumstance was in their flowing green hills and lush countryside that made this place look like a good idea? Three more days! Three more days aboard and they could have been rolling in lobsters and potatoes and kissing Anne of Green Gables."

I'm still not sure if he was joking or not.

We played many places on the island over the years. At UPEI, on the waterfront, in Rollo Bay, in Summerside, even at a miniature-buildings park called Woodleigh Replicas, I believe. We even helped usher in the controversial Confederation Bridge that links P.E.I. to the mainland of Canada. But the heart and soul of our time in P.E.I. lived at the Olde Dublin Pub, a small but very popular music pub in Charlottetown. A few of our friends had played there, and we were told we were perfect for the place, which had a reputation for being a rowdy drinking joint populated by locals and students in the winter and by tourists in the summer. The owner, Liam, a transplanted Irishman, ran the pub as organized and as clean and tidy as P.E.I. itself. The place has expanded a few times since we first played there more than twenty years ago, but back in the day the Olde Dublin could only be described as tiny, tucked into the top floor of a historic stone building in the heart of downtown. The wooden staircase came up in the centre of the room, and the bar, tables, and chairs were all tucked around it from stair rail to wall. At first glance I could not imagine how they could jam more than a few dozen people in there, and I was puzzled by the fact that I could see no obvious stage where a band might set up. Turns out they took out two of the tables against one wall and laid in a four-by-eight riser for the musicians to stand on.

We were no strangers to playing on cramped stages, but squeezing the four of us onto a riser that small would be a new challenge. We were four across the front, so we had twenty-four inches each to stand, each of us with an instrument and a mic stand. We rigged our set-up every way we could imagine, but no matter what we tried we just could not all be up there without someone getting the headstock of someone else's guitar in the face, or worse, the tip of Bob's fiddle bow in the eye. We had come this far and had no intention of having it not work. We noticed two empty milk crates and jammed them by the sides of the riser. For every set at the Olde Dublin Pub, the two guys on the ends, namely Bob and Darrell, had one foot on the stage and the other on a rickety milk crate doing their best to play, sing, and balance at the same time.

That first visit, we were to do a three-night stint—Thursday, Friday, and Saturday. Much like at the Lower Deck in Halifax, the crowd was fuelled by a dedicated group of Newfoundlanders and their converts. The pleasant Thursday night crowd swelled to a packed house on Saturday, with many familiar faces making a return visit.

The Olde Dublin was closed on Sundays. At home the pubs were crowded on Sunday afternoons, the only time most fishermen could have an afternoon drink. I got my first paid gig filling in for one of my uncles in his bar band playing the Sunday matinee.

How strange to be in Charlottetown, where bars and most restaurants were closed on the very day people could be out and about. I didn't know the half of it. People in P.E.I. took the day of rest *really* seriously. With the exception of the odd fast-food restaurant, pharmacy, gas station, and convenience store, everything in the entire province was shut. A day off for one was a day off for all.

Most notably, you could not buy alcohol of any kind, anywhere. Folks would devise complicated plans to sneak in the back doors of places to get a drink. It was like a provincial sport for the devilish few to get a Sunday buzz. When I explained to locals that in Newfoundland you could buy groceries and clothes on Sundays, one lady looked at me like I was a radical. When I mentioned that you could buy beer in the stores and that the pubs were open on Sunday, she looked at me like I was a Satanist.

I turned to Bob. "Are we more foolish than most people from P.E.I.?"

Bob, unfazed, answered, "Alan, we are more foolish than most people from everywhere."

P.E.I., I figured, is Newfoundland's sensible sister. Definitely from the same family, but nowhere near as wild. And she's more organized and way prettier, especially when she does herself up for visitors.

I can say this wholeheartedly: you would be hard pressed to find nicer people than folks of P.E.I. No shagging around or Hollywood daydreaming. If someone tells you he's gonna do something, you can be sure he's not kidding. Almost to a fault. And even in the most polite and orderly places, there are characters that manage to define and break the mould at the same time. Consider Roger.

It was late on night three at the Olde Dublin when I finally got around to chatting with the old skipper at the end of the bar.

He'd been there off and on each night, but was there for the entirety of Saturday's show. The stool at the end of the bar fit him perfectly.

"Yous fellas are drivin' 'er up there all weekend." I'd come to learn that "drivin' 'er" was about as good a compliment a band could get in these parts.

"Thank you, sir," I said, trying to show respect for a man quite a few years my senior.

"To hell with sir. On a Saturday night, I'm Roger," he said and extended a hand.

Now, I'd seen my share of worn and weathered hands on the fishermen in Petty Harbour, but Roger's hands were a different breed of beat-up. The skin on the hands I was used to was thinned near translucent with salt water. The skin on Roger's hands seemed thickened by layers of dirt and engine oil. Fishermen's hands were cut with knives and thin nets and lines. They were injured and marked in very specific places. Rather than decorated with individual cuts and lashes, Roger's hands were swollen and twisted all over.

I'd never seen anyone quite like him before. Roger's flesh was the colour of potatoes, with deep furrows running along his forehead and cheeks, as if you could grow root vegetables in the lines of his face.

"Always good when Liam gets the crowd in from Newfoundland. Some pile of singers over that way. Lotta fiddle players and dancers around here, but we got no singers like yous fellas."

I thanked him and added, "Works the other way, too, doesn't it? Tons of singers at home and a few accordion players, but we got no fiddle players like over here. And real step dancing at home is as rare as hens' teeth. We mostly sings songs and tries to get everyone in the room to sing them with us."

Roger nodded. "Yes, and that's what'll keep the people coming back. Keep them involved in it all and yous'll be all right, I figure."

After a bit more talk about the good times of the pub and the music, Roger offered me a pint, and I was grateful for it. "Enjoy it tonight, young fella, 'cause you won't get one tomorrow. Only place you're allowed to get a drink on the island tomorrow is from the chalice. Jesus, fellas be lining up to communion a dozen times if they could get away with it." He paused to look me up and down. "Of course, you can always get a little shine, if you happened to come across a fella who had some."

In the few days I'd been in P.E.I., I had heard about the moonshine tradition. Made total sense that a place built on potatoes would have shine stills, I supposed, but I told Roger I had not had any.

"Well, Sunday's the day to have a drop." He finished his pint in the third gulp. "Perhaps you'll get your chance." With that he patted me on the back and nipped away through the kitchen door.

That night, after the bar closed, the band was invited to a house party hosted by a bunch of Newfoundland students, and I felt both excited and strangely obliged to attend. The kitchen was jammed Newfoundland-style with college kids having a grand time, drinking and singing the odd song when cued by a fella from home with a guitar. We sang a few tunes and drank a few too many beers. Around six in the morning, I landed on a fold-up cot closest to the door in a two-bed, two-cot room with three other fellas, in an inn on a hill I still could not find, and fell sound asleep.

I bolted upright after what felt like ten seconds. A single but definite knock on the door like a gunshot. I was dazed and reached for my glasses. Just as the glasses hit my nose, a second knock hit the door.

I stumbled to my feet as Bob wondered who the frig it could be. I pulled open the door, and all I could see was a silhouette bathed in the stark glare of the sun.

"Jesus, you're still in bed? It's after eight o'clock."

My eyes adjusted enough for me to recognize the man before me. Roger. Dressed in his Sunday best.

He lifted a mason jar into the light. It was filled with clear liquid. "Manager at the pub told me you were here so I figured I'd drop off a bit of that shine you were looking for before mass."

Before I could say a single word to the man, I was holding a jar of moonshine. I opened my mouth to say thank you, but only dry air and squeaks came out. I nodded instead, and Roger went on.

"Makes that myself, see. On the sly. Top secret," he explained, and then slightly contradicted himself with, "Fellas lined up by the garage doors every Sunday for a drop."

I smiled a thank-you as I still could not speak, raised the jar to Roger, and started to close the door. Through my sleepy eyes, I noticed disappointment drift across his face. I'd made that expression myself enough times to know it meant "Oh, I thought you were going to ask me in for a drink." So, standing in the doorway of a room in an inn on some imagined hill in Charlottetown, with a gent in a suit and me wearing only my underwear, I did the polite thing I was raised to do. I opened the door wide and stepped aside with an arm gesturing towards the cot closest to the door.

Roger smiled a smile as big as I figured he could smile and stepped proudly and gratefully into the hotel room. Two of my bandmates in the beds did not stir. Only Bob on the other cot moaned as he realized we were now hosts to a charming bootlegger at eight o'clock on a Sunday morning. He rolled over, faced the wall, and pretended to be asleep.

"Jesus, this crowd is still asleep!" Roger seemed honestly surprised, but he did not so much as break stride as he came to take his place next to me on the squeaky cot. "Now, you might find that stuff a bit strong, especially if you're just out of bed, but once you gets the taste of it, there's nothing better in the world to wake you up."

It just then occurred to me that I would have to drink some of this stuff. I tried to verbalize that I might try it later, but I just coughed. I felt Roger gently lift the jar from my hands.

"I'll get that started for yous. Ye mandolin players don't always have the strongest grip." And with that he twisted off the lid and took a gulp of the clear liquid, closed his eyes to enjoy it going down, then handed the jar back to me.

I figured it must not be that bad, as my new bedmate had just necked about four ounces of it without so much as a grimace, so I put the jar to my lips.

I felt it before I tasted it. My lips and tongue burned as the heat paved the way for the fire to follow. The hairs in my nose recoiled and warned of a clear and present danger, but I was too far gone to stop now. I poured about a thimbleful into my mouth.

I have never eaten fire, or put a lit flare on my tongue. I have never wrapped my lips around a BBQ lighter and clicked it on. I have never taken hot embers from the woodstove and sucked them like candy. But I cannot imagine how any of these acts could have burned more than sipping a teaspoon of this liquor. If hell has a shooter, it must surely be this booze.

I was expending so much energy not spitting out the moonshine that somehow my face remained expressionless. Roger interpreted this as approval.

"Yes, see, some fellas screw their faces right up when they gets the first taste, eh? Find it kind of strong, I suppose. But yous are like myself, I'd say, and don't mind a strong drink at all."

He waited for me to confirm his evaluation by taking another, longer swig. So I did.

You know that trick when you shoot tequila and try to put it right in your throat so you won't really taste it? Doesn't work, does it? No, it does not. Quite often in fact it has the opposite effect, as I was now experiencing on the bed, my mouth full of obnoxious devil juice and my throat closing over as if my body knew better than my foolish brain.

Roger looked doubtful. Some primal Petty Harbour pride in me swelled up and I knew I could not let this man down. I took a breath through my nose and swallowed hard.

Is it possible certain alcohol can skip your stomach and go immediately into your bloodstream? I have never injected alcohol, but I can't imagine the booze in the syringe gets into you any quicker than Roger's moonshine. The moment it went down I felt its effects. My temperature rose five degrees in a second. Roger winked a very Newfoundland wink as he took the jar from my hand and tipped it till it was almost two-thirds gone.

He stood and brushed off his suit jacket and left the jar on the floor by the cot. "Perhaps them other fellas might want to try some when they comes around later on." He checked his hair in the mirror on the wall and made for the door. He was about to go when he paused and a look of concern came over him. "Yous knows where the church is, right?" He surveyed the room of sleeping, pretending-to-be-sleeping, and barely awake fellas in their drawers. "Ye can't be missing mass."

I just shook my head, which was now almost completely consumed by the shine.

"But I suppose yous crowd went to the Saturday evening service?" Roger said, perhaps to convince himself that he could now walk out guilt free.

I just nodded, and I touched my nose in that "you got it" kind of way.

"See yous down the road," Roger said, and let the door click closed behind him.

I lay my head back on the pillow and felt the moonshine speeding through my body. I had never gone from sober to smashed quite so quickly in my life. Here in a place where alcohol was strictly forbidden on the holiest day of the week, sitting in my underwear on a cot in a hotel room, I had shared a drink or two with a strange man who I met in a bar the night before. He slipped into our room, got me drunk in my drawers, and left without my saying so much as a word. And all before Sunday church services had even started.

Mom would be so proud.

WORST SEAT EVER

It had been a long run, one of our first off Newfoundland. We had played thirty-one of the past thirty-three nights in various pubs and campuses around Nova Scotia, New Brunswick, and P.E.I. All the shows were at least two sets, and many of them three and even four. The last night of the tour was a burn-the-house-down ripper at the Olde Dublin Pub, and we had celebrated into the wee hours. After a drive and the ferry and a drive, we arrived back at Halifax airport in various states of disarray, cleanliness, and sobriety. Those who were better in one category were most likely suffering in the others as we poured into YHZ to catch a plane home.

The woman working the Air Nova check-in counter sized up us and our equipment the way she might have looked at a minor-league semi-pro hockey team after a weekend tournament and late-night shenanigans: lots of eye-rolling and head-shaking, but just enough smiles, glances, and flirt to let you know you were not completely without your charms.

"You might not get all that gear on the Dash, but we'll do our best for you. Go quick now, all of you, to Gate 6."

"On the Dash?" I wondered out loud.

Bob, a much more seasoned traveller than me, looked pissed. "Like flying in a hair dryer."

These days, you can easily get larger jet service to most destinations in Atlantic Canada, but in the early nineties, Air Canada's affiliate Air Nova regularly flew smaller Dash 8s from Halifax to St. John's. These nearly indestructible planes remain a favourite of commercial airlines around the world, as they are extremely reliable and inexpensive to run. "Roomy" and "incredibly quiet" are phrases I've never heard used to describe a Dash 8.

We made our way to the gate. As I would quickly come to learn, it is almost impossible to sit at the gate of any airplane in any airport heading to St. John's and not see someone you not only recognize but know on a first-name basis. You could be in Toronto, Montreal, New York, or London, and within 150 metres of the gate for the St. John's flight, you'd be chatting with a cousin or someone you knew in high school. And, of course, Darrell always had a buddy.

"Power!" some fella with a nickname like Fish, Sneakers, or Gutz might shout as we approached.

"What are ya at, Gutz, b'y?" Darrell would answer. "You up on the mainland making a fortune again, I s'pose."

"No, b'y, spent almost all my cheque on women and beer. And I wasted the rest." Gutz would wink, "Headin' home, b'ys?"

Or something like that.

On this morning the chats and greetings were muted, as we were mostly exhausted and hungry for home. As we made our way across the tarmac to the plane, I stumbled a little as I almost fell asleep on my feet. The rest of the guys were no more spry than me.

We made our way up the three short steps and into the small aircraft. Right away, one of the fellas under his breath said, "Ah, no f—king way!"

"What's up?" I asked.

"A missus and a baby in the seat next to me down there. Look." He was almost weeping into his boarding pass. "I gotta sleep or I'm gonna barf." I thought he might lose it right there next to the attractive young flight attendant.

"Is there a problem, boys?" asked Andrea, so her Air Nova nametag read.

"No, it's cool," I said to her. I looked to my bandmate, almost asleep on his feet. "I'll switch with you, man. I can sleep on a clothesline."

"You sure?"

"Yeah, nothing to it."

I turned to Andrea with a raised eyebrow that asked if this switch was cool.

"Very nice of you." She smiled.

"Thanks, man. Get you next time," my tired friend whispered and slumped into my seat next to one of the other fellas in the band who had boarded earlier and was already sound asleep. It was not meant to be a big deal. Nothing more than a small favour of the sort others had done and would do for me dozens of times.

I went to his seat next to the lady and the baby. I had the seat on the aisle, and she and the not-so-wee fella were in by the window. I nodded and was about to sit when she spoke.

"Oh Jesus, honey, will you sit in here? I hates flying and I dare say I'll be in and out of that bathroom like a yo-yo. I hope they got lots of them throw-up bags too, 'cause my guts are churning here."

"Yeah, sure, whatever you like."

She smiled, stood, and hugged me. Hard. Squeezing the baby between us. "Jesus, how nice is it to be going home where people are friggin' nice."

I swear I felt the baby push us apart as he flexed in just his diaper and T-shirt. As we were switching seats, his face met mine nose to nose. I can't say if it was that he was just squat up against me, or that his lady had shown me some affection, or some sixth baby instinct, but one thing was uncomfortably obvious right away. He did not like me. Not one bit.

The lady, who identified herself as Joan, said that her five-month-old son, TJ, was most likely the son of a great big fella from Alberta. I thought I understood what she meant by "most likely," but perhaps I didn't. In any case, that baby was a brute, more of a man than me. Baby face on a head as big as a paint can. Bald—not like a head that hair would later grow on, but like a mid-life Viking whose hair had thinned and receded so much that he said shag it and shaved off the last few remnants of his younger days. I swear I saw the start of a moustache, and I am not exaggerating in the slightest to suggest he had biceps. Big ones.

TJ eyeballed me. Not curious, but challenging. I returned his glare, but he did not blink. At all. I looked away and assumed the haze of my morning was confusing me. When I looked back, his stare was, if anything, more intense. He was steeled like a boxer at the centre of the squared circle while the referee explains that he wants a clean flight.

It was on. And he was winning.

"Everything okay here?" Andrea asked. I guessed she was fairly new to the job. Her surely new, spotless uniform was perfectly pressed, and her red-and-white scarf was neatly tied around her long and slender neck. Her golden hair was pulled back into a bun so flawless that it spoke of her attention to detail and professionalism. I did not want to dwell on what she might have thought of me with my ripped denim jacket, four-day-old shirt, and jeans so dirty they could walk home by themselves.

"Yeah, we're cool." I did not want to lose whatever gains I had made.

Andrea looked to Joan. "You are flying with an infant, ma'am. Are you aware of the security procedures for the safety of you and your child?"

"Is there an open bar?" Joan answered.

"Uh, yes, ma'am, there will be a beverage cart after takeoff, but I need to know if—"

"All I needs to know is if I got to pay for drinks or not. And yes, I'll manage TJ as best I can and I got buddy here to help me. He some friggin' nice, sure, let me sit on the outside already. I could kiss him, sure, he's so nice. Probably will too before this flight's over, especially if the drinks are free, hey, b'y." Joan elbowed me so hard I grunted. And quick as a flash, TJ grunted back at me, squinting his eyes so hard there were lines in his forehead.

Andrea opened her eyes wide to me, then went to her seat at the front of the plane.

As we sped down the runway, I watched the propellers of the Dash 8 spin so quickly they disappeared from sight. I felt the wheels leave the ground and I felt the weightlessness that comes the moment an aircraft goes from rolling to flying. But as we made our way to the clouds, my peace was broken by Joan's whispered exclamation.

"F—k you, mainland. Hope I never sets foot on you again." She waited until I turned my head and nodded awkwardly before continuing. "Bunch a savages up here, aren't they? Can't wait to get home where people are not a bunch a ignorant pricks like they are up here. Cut your throat for a nickel, wouldn't they?"

She waited for a response.

"I had a pretty good time, actually," I said a bit sheepishly.

"Well, you must be the luckiest bastard ever walked on two legs. No wonder you're so nice. Hold on to him while I takes a whiz, will ya?"

"Uh, I think we've got to wait till the seat belt sign is—"

She swung the small manchild onto my lap and bolted for the washroom. I saw Andrea shake her head.

TJ squirmed and kicked on my lap as he faced the seat in front of me. His heel connected with my shin so hard I thought it would leave a bruise, so I figured I should spin him around to face me. I lifted him, with all the effort my exhausted, morning-after-the-night-before body could muster, and half dropped him straddling one of my legs as again we were face to face. I thought he might be upset by the swinging and dropping, but he still held the same cold, unblinking stare.

"Hey, buddy," I whispered, and offered a friendly smile.

His eyes opened a little wider and I saw the first traces of a break in this standoff. One corner of his mouth turned up ever so slightly, and his eyes blinked three or four long, relaxing blinks.

"That a fella." But as the last word left my mouth, I learned his look was not one of peace but one of relief. I felt warm liquid run down my thigh and into my crotch as an unmistakable whiff wafted up to my nose. I instinctively lifted him off my lap and held him up a few inches until were eye to eye. I could hear the trickle now, and his gaze never left mine. He was pissing on me. But it was no accident.

There wasn't room to get him between my legs and on the floor, and I couldn't reach the aisle to get him out there, so I just held him there in mid-air, pee leaking out through a loose and soggy diaper, running down his dangling leg and off his big toe, so perfectly pointed that I swore he was aiming it, quite accurately, at my jeans.

"That little bastard!" Joan, back from her surprisingly short visit to the can, grabbed her son. "What a mess he got made on you. I was hoping to get him home without changing that soggy diaper, but I'm going to have to."

Andrea finally could take no more. "Ma'am, the seat belt light is still on. Please take your seat and we'll deal with it all when the captain says it's safe to move around the cabin."

"Oh yes, I s'pose. Sorry 'bout that," she whispered mock-politely and took her seat, then laid TJ back in my lap. "You got it on you now, sure. What odds about a bit more, hey, b'y?"

I was about to protest when the seat belt light went dim. During Andrea's "the captain has turned off the seat belt light" speech, Joan jumped up and grabbed a large purse from the overhead compartment and dropped it on her seat. As TJ's pee cooled on me, I watched her root through makeup, cigarettes, and what could have been underwear to pull out a small changing pad, which she placed on her seat, a clean diaper, and a tube of Wet Ones.

"All right," she said, "pass him over."

"There's usually a change table in the washroom." I hoped this would shift her plan.

"Nah, sure this is best kind." She knelt in the aisle, popped TJ onto the pad, and dropped the seatback tray to use as a shelf for supplies. She whipped off the diaper like a bruiser in a hockey fight tearing off his combatant's jersey. The smell of baby pee was quickly replaced with the stench of baby poop. She dropped the diaper half-open on the tray above TJ, whose arms were flailing and legs kicking. He was smiling a toothless full smile now. In the midst of his stretching and reaching, his mighty baby arm struck the soiled diaper on the tray and sent it flying. I tracked it as if it was moving in slow motion. It followed a perfect arc through the air, unfolding as it passed the midpoint and dropping, poop side down, perfectly onto my lap.

The warmth of the number two reheating the cooling number one.

Andrea, in her perfectly pressed uniform, her PA speech now complete, stood in the aisle over Joan. Her gentle hand was covering her open mouth. A strand of her hair dropped from her no longer flawless bun.

Joan looked up at Andrea's wide-eyed gape. "What's wrong with you, princess? You never saw a dirty arse before, I s'pose."

Andrea just shook her head and pointed to me and my knee pad.

Joan seemed to notice for the first time. "Oh Jesus, honey, sorry about that. He's always grabbing for the dirty diapers. What's wrong with him, at all?"

She tried to pluck the diaper from my thigh, but the contents were gluing it in place now and she had to give it a good tug before it came loose. It must have been near reusable because all the contents seemed to still be on my leg.

"Hold on, honey, I gets us a wipe." Joan tossed me the tube of Wet Ones, and while she fixed up TJ, I corralled the shite off my leg and into as good a Wet Ones wrapper as I could muster.

By the time I finished, Andrea was standing over me wearing rubber gloves and an apron, holding a roll of paper towels and a garbage bag. A few more hairs had dropped, and her scarf was coming untied. "I'm so sorry about this." I could tell she really was.

Joan looked up at her. "I think he deserves a drink, don't you?"

Before I could say something like, "No thanks, I've been drinking for about a month now, so I think I'll just sit here soberly and enjoy the pee and poop," Andrea ran off. She returned with two cold cans of beer.

"You can leave them for him, but I likes rum and Coke. Strong, too. No good bringing only one a them little bottles."

Andrea soon returned with two small Captain Morgan minis, a can of Coke, and a glass of ice. Joan rested TJ on her lap and made room for the quickly growing bar. When Andrea left to serve others, I said quietly to Joan, "Hey, I don't really want these beers." I meant that we could probably return them.

"More for me," she said. She slid one of the cans into her giant purse and very dexterously opened the other with one hand. She took a long, slow slug and handed the can to TJ, his man-hands easily managing to keep it steady. "Don't drink that, now. Just hold it while I mixes my rum and Coke."

She went to work opening one of the rums and pouring it and some Coke over the ice. Her long arms were wrapped around TJ, who held the open can of beer at his chest. He looked down the hole and saw the liquid. Then, turning towards me with the same cold-as-ice look, he reached out and tipped the can bottom up, pouring the whole works of it over my leg.

I yelped as the cold beer cooled the poop stain that had warmed the pee stain that earlier had cooled in the very same spot.

"Jesus, honey, you scared the life out of me." As Joan lifted her hand to draw her blouse together and cover her heart—the universal sign of shock for Newfoundland women—her arm bumped her rum and Coke, tipping it on the tray. The cocktail ran over the edge onto the beer on my lap. The ice followed, and my leg, hip, twig, and berries were all instantly frozen.

Seconds later, Joan was dabbing and pawing at my leg and private parts with a handful of Wet Ones. TJ was shaking with laughter.

I noticed Andrea up front in her seat facing us with her head in her hands now as she sat, leaning forward, her elbows pressing into her legs. Through her fingers I could see her eyes wider than ever with disbelief. Her scarf was completely untied now, and her uniform wrinkling fast.

Joan settled for the next while and enjoyed the second beer and second rum and Coke while TJ relaxed into her and, at last, fell asleep. The little fella actually looked peaceful for a half-hour or so. But he woke quickly and loudly.

His waking cry was a mad battle cry from an ancient warrior before he leaps from his horse into combat with swords and arrows flying. He yelled as loud as an adult who'd just had his legs broken.

"He's starved now, guaranteed." Joan dug around in the enormous purse and pulled out a bottle. She had it ready to go and just had to shake it a bit and then take off the cap and flip over the nipple from inside the lid. She was halfway through this procedure when TJ swung his arms about his mom's face, striking the open bottle of formula and spilling it over himself, her, and eventually, of course, me.

"Oh for the love of Jesus, TJ! Now look what you're after going and doing!"

TJ responded with his same battle cry, and Joan rolled her eyes.

"I thought I was done with this foolishness, but that was the last bottle, so you're gonna get what you wants, you sucky little fella."

Was she talking to me? I really hoped not, because as she spoke she undid three buttons on her blouse, revealing a bra like I'd never seen before. It had a zipper around the cup, and no sooner did I notice it than she unzipped and whipped out a pointy, stiff boob. I tried to look away but couldn't. It looked right back at me, its single brown eye swollen and unblinking.

TJ saw it, too, and dove at it like a kid bobbing for apples, his eyes as wide open as his mouth. He was on it and sucking hard within seconds.

Joan actually winked at me. "Jesus, honey, you're getting some show out of it, aren't ya? Lucky bastard."

I turned my head back to Andrea, who had now pulled most of the hair out of her bun. Her scarf lay on the floor beside her.

TJ settled in peacefully and Joan relaxed back into it all. "He's getting a nice flow there now." Which I thought was more info than necessary.

The seat belt light came on and the captain announced we were making our descent into St. John's.

As the plane veered north, I saw the spray from a whale just off Cape Spear.

"Whales are still blowing." I meant to just think it, but in my exhaustion I must've said it out loud. Joan instantly undid her seat belt and stood baby on teat and dove over me, pressing her face to the window.

"Whales! I loves whales. Look, TJ. Mommy told ya we'd see whales!" She grabbed her son's head, plucked it from her breast, and turned it to the window. He just looked at me with the same cold stare. I would have stared back but my attention was diverted by a long, skinny squirt of white coming right for my chin. It struck home. Then another a heartbeat later. I honestly did not know what was happening.

TJ did. He grinned as he watched the milk from his mother's breast leak four or five more times and strike me on the chin and chest and run down onto my jacket and crotch, another sickly smell wafting through the air.

Andrea came running towards us. "Ma'am. You *have* to take your seat. This is not safe for you or your baby! And we are land—" Her words stopped as she saw Joan's gorged breast hanging out of her zipper bra and pointing directly at my chin and leaking milk all over the place. "OH. MY. GOD," was all she could say, and she knelt on the aisle floor, holding back tears, I think.

"All right, girl. Jesus, don't have a fit. I'm just trying to show the little fella a whale."

In what can only be described as a state of utter filth, I watched Robin Hood Bay and Outer Cove slip past the window as we neared the runway. Just for a few seconds before the wheels hit the ground, the small plane's descent became more like falling than flying. It is the point where it's tough not to face the hard truth that this is not a magic trick at all. You are in a metal tube with wings plummeting to an asphalt pad at hundreds of kilometres per hour. The Dash 8 touched down.

Home.

"Yay!" Joan smiled at TJ and he smiled back. "I told you. Nothing to it." She stood and looked to me. She turned and walked down the aisle. As she disappeared up the gangway, I saw TJ eyeballing me through the crowd.

By the time I peeled myself from the window seat, my bandmate who I'd switched seats with was by my side, with an apologetic look on his face and a hand over his nose to keep out my stench.

"Dude, I owe you one. Or ten."

"It's all good." I almost meant it, as I stepped to exit the plane, but was met by Andrea. Her hair was unkempt now and her uniform wrinkled and soiled by the constant ferrying of booze, diapers, and garbage to and from our seats. She was stressed and exhausted, and I may have noticed the beginnings of a tear in her eye.

"It's all good, girl. I wasn't that clean to start with," I said as she pointed open-mouthed to Joan and shook her head. I spoke again as Andrea seemed like she could not. "Just another Newfoundlander trying to make their way home. Same as me."

"I am so sorry about this."

And she meant it as a few weeks later I got a letter in the mail from the VP of customer service of Air Canada offering a free flight for having "undergone emotional trauma and physical discomfort while accommodating a difficult passenger." I couldn't decide if they meant Joan or TJ.

I made my way to baggage claim, where my then fairly new girlfriend (and now wife) was waiting for me. When Joanne had kissed me goodbye for my first big tour on the mainland, she must have wondered what kind of state I'd be in when I returned. As I rounded the corner, she looked like a person who'd just realized her worries had been warranted. My smell reached her long before I did. I did not bother to go for a hug or kiss, for it would have been as unhealthy as it was unwelcomed.

She spoke through a hand masking her nose and mouth. "Alan? What in God's name is on you?"

"Not much," I said casually. "Just pee, poop, beer, rum, Coke, baby formula, and, ah, oh yeah . . . breast milk."

NEW BRUNSWICK

F our giggling Newfoundlanders standing shoulder to shoulder on the side of the highway.

Peeing.

Uphill.

That is what many people driving just off Highway 2 near Moncton, New Brunswick, saw late, late one Friday night. We had just played a gig at Université de Moncton and were headed out of town when we saw the sign for the famous tourist attraction. No one actually planned what we were going to do. But I think we all knew exactly what would go down. Or, rather, up.

Magnetic Hill sits just outside Moncton. This and the few other places like it on earth are understood to be optical illusions, as your eyes are tricked by rising and falling terrain and it appears objects can roll uphill. It is a common family vacation destination where the thing to do is stop at the "bottom" of the hill and put your car in neutral. Slowly but surely your car will roll forward, and by every reference your eyes and brain can muster, you will indeed be rolling uphill. We wanted to experience it for ourselves, so we turned off the Trans-Canada towards Mountain Road in search of magic. It was cool enough, but the sensation was probably muted a bit by the darkness. It left us all wanting a more memorable experience.

So we parked the car on the shoulder of the road, ran back to the middle of the hill, and dropped our drawers. Side by each, four white Newfoundland bums shone in passing headlights to cheers and barmps as four pee streams fell to the shoulder of the road and immediately turned uphill. Our knees buckled and bodies shook as we laughed as hard as I can remember with tears in our eyes and birds in our hands.

Magnetic Hill was one of a few things I knew about New Brunswick before we first made our way to play there. I knew that Saint John was a city that practically shared its name with the city I lived in but was spelled quite differently. I would not be able to count for you how many times I've heard someone from central or western North America confuse St. John's and Saint John. In the early nineties I met a hero-band of mine from B.C. who shall remain nameless. I explained how excited I was to meet them and how much I would have loved to see them live as a teenager in St. John's. The singer insisted they had played the city's hockey rink in 1986. "Yeah, for sure, man, I remember it like it was yesterday. We played Halifax and packed up the trucks and rolled to St. John's to play the next night."

"Really? With the ferry and all? Sounds impossible," I said, but he stuck to his convictions.

"Yeah, for sure, we didn't take the ferry, we drove overnight and made it no problem . . ." His voice started to trail off as the truth of which Atlantic city he had actually played dawned on him. "Oh . . . right. That wasn't Newfoundland at all, was it."

Just this week, a friend of mine organizing a hair-colouring conference in Newfoundland tried to help two delegates from North
Carolina rebook their flights. They had looked up a St. John's–
sounding place in Atlantic Canada and booked tickets into Saint
John. Been happening for years. Not even Google Maps and the
internet can quell the confusion. Come to think of it, why wouldn't
they be confused? Why have two cities in the same region of one
country with the same name? Makes no sense, until you remember St. John's, Newfoundland, and Saint John, New Brunswick,
were in different countries less than a generation ago.

I also knew that there was a place in New Brunswick where
tides were a big deal. And I confess this confused me greatly.
"Come marvel at the mystery, beauty, and power of some of the
highest tides in the world," tourism ads and TV commercials
would proclaim. As a kid, I remember sitting at home in Petty
Harbour wondering what could possibly be the attraction of
rising and falling tides. That very thing happened every single
day just outside my window. Twice a day, in fact. In my announcer
voice I would perform my very own commercials for my brother
and sisters: "Come see the incredible tides here in Petty Harbour.
Note how at low tide the entire wharf ladder is completely accessible to man, woman, and child alike. Yet at high tide the fourth
and fifth steps of the wharf ladder are completely submerged.
Incredible!" The whole thing seemed so ridiculous to me.

About the only other thing I knew about New Brunswick was
that a number of people in the province were French speakers,
including one of my sister Kim's heart throbs, Roch Voisine.

When Great Big Sea started touring there early in 1994, the
first thing I noticed about New Brunswick was that it has three
cities. It is the only Atlantic province that can make such a claim.
Before you rush to Google to prove me wrong, consider that on

that early trip to New Brunswick, I would have defined a city as a place with a true downtown and a population of approximately twenty thousand or more. Other provinces, like Nova Scotia, might boast multiple urban centres—Halifax, Dartmouth, Sydney. Even Newfoundlanders would jump to argue for St. John's, Mount Pearl, Corner Brook, and Labrador City. But these folks would have to eventually agree that the only province with three separate and distinct downtowns is New Brunswick. Moncton, Fredericton, and Saint John are all real, honest-to-God cities of more than twenty thousand people. Of course at the time, the most important thing to us about a province with three cities was the possibility of three big gigs within a short drive of each other. And we would want to do all three.

Moncton is not the capital of New Brunswick, but it felt like it should be as its urban downtown core impressed me instantly. Its worldly music scene seemed to have a lot to do with the fact that it is a truly bilingual city that neatly runs along the Petitcodiac River. Just about everyone I met was completely bilingual. No one seemed to have a first language or a second language. French people all spoke English fluently, and vice versa. At no point did they seem to be translating before speaking. Often, it seemed to me they were speaking both English and French at the same time.

"Donnez-moi a hotdog," I swore I heard someone say at the street-meat cart late one night on Main. I wondered if, as well as fluently speaking two languages, they may have invented a third.

If you were to watch a traditional music group from Moncton set up, you could be forgiven for assuming it was much like a group from Newfoundland. The lineup and instrumentation at first glance is near identical, with acoustic guitars, mandolins, accordions, and fiddles. But when they count un, deux, trois, quatre, there is no mistaking you are in an entirely different musical world. The French songs were exotic to me, but it was the way they played their instruments that seemed truly unique. The fingers of the fiddlers and accordion players flew over their instruments. So many notes played at blistering tempo with tremendous flare. And for ensemble music, there was a reckless individuality among the players.

And then there were their feet. These folks sat and step danced at the same time. The percussion and energy of their perfectly timed heel stomps and toe taps drove tunes that were already flying up to a whole new gear. I'd never seen anything like it.

Driving into Saint John in the early 1990s, it was tough not to stare at an abandoned derelict building that dominated the skyline. Silhouetted against the sky, with its broken bricks and graffiti-laden walls it looked as much like a horror film set as it did the condemned hospital that it was.

The city was in transition. The stone buildings that stretched up and down the steep hills around the harbour were all being repurposed from an industrial function to whatever was to come next for them. Along the harbour itself, I could see the beginnings of a walkway like the one in Halifax. The scary hospital on the hill was demolished by the second or third time I walked the Saint John streets and I wondered if I'd ever seen a town transform so quickly.

By the time GBS got a slot at one of the most sought-after festivals in Atlantic Canada, Festival by the Sea, in Saint John, we were becoming a thing. We'd been offered an afternoon slot, and as the gig approached, we kept getting slid up the bill. By the time show day rolled around, we were the de facto headliner of the day. Their usual crowd of hundreds grew to thousands, and the line at the autograph tent after our set stretched around the site.

As a teenager in the eighties, I was completely hypnotized by hair metal music videos on MuchMusic. I figured signing boobs and the like was a normal part of being a rock star, and eventually I'd be at it all the time. So when the boys and I were asked to sign autographs at the Festival by the Sea, and when a lovely gal in her early twenties walked up to the table and leaned in with a devilish look in her eye and said, "I love your voice. Would you sign my leg?" I felt like I had reached the Promised Land. I sprang to my feet and said in my best casual voice, like it was no big deal, "Yeah, sure, if you like."

I can't say what I was expecting exactly. Perhaps I had visions of her seductively lifting her high-heel shoe to the table and slipping the key of her hotel suite into my hand, like in the Bon Jovi video. Or maybe I pictured her, just like Tawny Kitaen on the car in the Whitesnake video, writhing in satisfaction when my Sharpie touched her flesh. I honestly can't recall which teenage fantasy I thought was about to play out in the crowded merchandise tent that day. I can tell you I was not expecting her to reach down and lift her prosthetic limb to the table, the weight of the heavy wooden foot making a loud bang as it hit.

"Jesus Christ!" I shouted and jumped back.

She cracked up laughing and so did just about everyone else in the tent. So much for being David Coverdale. Even for a moment.

Fredericton is arguably the prettiest of the three New Brunswick cities. The road into town stretches along a beautiful river lined with trees, and the heart of the downtown is nestled in between them. Great times there at a few pubs, and mostly at the university and eventually the Playhouse theatre. We even played the Aitken Centre hockey rink, and survived a blackout mid-show by having the crowd of thirty-five hundred light the place with cigarette lighters and sing a song a cappella together.

One Fredericton gig was most memorable for the route we took to get there. For younger readers, it should be noted that back in the days before everyone had a high-speed, globally connected computer in their pocket, we relied on maps and atlases to get us from one place to another. These nationally produced publications were often quite accurate for Southern Ontario and other large urban centres, but not so much for the nooks and crannies of Atlantic Canada. So we relied as much on word of mouth, argument, and rumour. Sleepy and coffee-starved, I might try to recall the exact details of a post-gig conversation with a well-served pub patron hiding in the haze of the late night.

"Buddy said, if the lobster trucks are not running towards Digby, you can take two hours off the trip to Saint John by cutting through MacDuncan's Farm Road just outside of Annapolis Royal. Now, you can't do that if it's Tuesday because they runs the sheep on Tuesdays, or if it's rainy because the road gets mucky from the apple fields. Other than them two times, you can dart through there, for sure. Like I said, unless the lobster trucks are running." My hands waved directions in the air as Bob surveyed the map from the front passenger seat, trying to make any sense of what I was going on about.

These secret barroom shortcuts rarely worked, but there was this road, which I believe is now identified as Highway 112, that runs north of the main highway between Moncton and Fredericton. We'd heard that if you take this northern back road, you can shave almost thirty minutes off the drive between the two cities, and we were all about saving time, so we turned onto the two-lane road heading west towards the town of Hunters Home en route to Fredericton, the large green-and-white *Welcome to Moncton* sign disappearing in the distance behind us.

We did not check the map to see if this road was legit. We were delighted to be in on the secret. When you spend forty hours a week in a minivan, you are always up for making it new and exciting in any way possible. The road was lined with thick woods and farm fields, and as it was well into fall, the trees shone bright orange and red on the north and south sides all the way along. It was all beautifully the same everywhere we looked.

About eighty kilometres into this pleasant drive, we saw a most quaint gas bar and tourist shop. "We're way ahead of time—let's stop and check it out," I said, always eager to step on fresh ground.

We circled the small building but realized we were driving the wrong way to enter the gas pump, so we turned again and spun back to the front of the shop, where a gent was waiting by the pump.

We all peed and got a paper and a drink and loaded back in the van. Tony, our sound man, tour manager, and driver, paused at the shoulder of the road and looked left and right a couple of times, for a moment longer than he usually did. I figured he was just being extra careful on the unfamiliar road.

For the next forty-five minutes or so, we drove past the same beautiful colours and fields. Finally, Bob broke the spell, his sunglasses resting on his red forehead, squinting at the spinning map in his hands. "We've been driving on this road for an hour and a half. Shouldn't we be seeing signs for Fredericton?"

"Yeah," Tony said. "Nice enough road, but so much for a shortcut."

And then we saw it.

Just ahead, at the junction of Highway 112 and the main highway, a large green-and-white sign screamed *Welcome to Moncton*.

Five grown-up, awake fellas drove about eighty kilometres in the wrong direction in broad daylight and not one of us had noticed. We turned right onto the main highway and drove into Fredericton while silently formulating arguments about who should be blamed for the shag-up that made us ninety minutes late.

We would spend the better part of two years going in and out of the three cities of New Brunswick and surely came to look forward to each trip. New Brunswick, I supposed, is Newfoundland's quiet cousin. She gets very little air-time at the supper table, but is way more complex and fascinating than you might have thought.

I was staying at the Beauséjour Hotel in the middle of downtown Moncton, and had gone to a party in another hotel down the road. It was an after-party of sorts, and I was feeling like a rock star when I left to walk back up the road to my hotel. As there was a lovely trail by the Petitcodiac River, I decided this would do just fine. But as the lights of the hotel faded, I realized I'd got turned around when I left the party. I was on a dark trail very late at night—early morning, actually—by myself. My safe-traveller instincts kicked in and my senses heighted.

A few steps more and I distinctly heard a sound behind me. I spun around, but found no one on the path. Must be the whisky or the full moon playing tricks on me. Two more steps and I definitely heard something approaching, closer now. I picked up my pace to get ahead of it, but with every step, the sound got closer. I was going to have to face whoever or whatever it was.

I steeled myself and spun around. Again there was no one to be seen.

The sound was not coming from the path, I realized, but from the river itself. There, in a straight line across the river, a wave pushed against the flow, ever closer to me.

I blinked a couple of times to mark what seemed like some kind of Old Testament tale. The river appeared to have changed its mind and was running backwards. The water churned as the wave pushed its way up the river from the sea. It was as if the earth had tipped ever so slightly and the ocean had to level itself and there was not a single human thing that could ever be done about it, except sit and watch it.

Unstoppable. Humbling.

And just like the ads I'd scoffed at as a kid had said, I stood there and marvelled at the mystery, beauty, and power of some of the highest tides in the world.

SUPPER

"**O**h yes, my dear, the youngsters are all home and they are all grand, sure."

Mom is on the phone in the kitchen. I am watching her from the inside chair at the table with my back to the wall. One might wonder why I sat there, considering there is no one at any other of the more easily accessible chairs on the outside of the table. But this is my chair. It has always been my chair. Inside. Back to the wall. Brother Bernie's chair against the wall to my right, and Dad's at the head of the table to my left. Mom's directly across from me with my sister Michelle's chair to her left and sister Kim's chair next to Michelle's at the foot of the table. And though the rest of the family are all in the living room chatting or milling about the house, I was drawn by habit or default or both to my usual spot at home.

As ever, the kitchen smells like gravy and freshly made bread. Eight loaves are cooling on a cloth on top of the deep freeze while a pot of beef gravy steams and bubbles on one burner of the stove. Another pot, filled with potatoes, boils hard on a second burner, and yet another filled to the brim with carrot, turnips, cabbage, and salt meat boils even harder on a third. Between me and the stove, the same simple table of my childhood is set for Sunday dinner. The same table that I did my homework on and hid under as a ten-year-old to watch Uncle Leonard play fancy guitar chords well past my bedtime. Same chairs my brother Bernie punctured with his pocket knife not five minutes after getting it for his birthday. As ever, no fancy china or finery. Just six well-worn knives, scratched and nicked next to six forks showing their age, bent out of and bent back into shape time and time again. Just like the rest of us.

I watch Mom chat with a cigarette in one hand and the phone pressed to her ear in a stance she has perfected over the years. She has one leg lifted and is half sitting on the counter, half standing on the floor. A warrior's pose of sorts. Strong. Immovable. She holds the cigarette close to her mouth to be ready for a time when my aunt will start talking and she can get a quick draw in. She might be lucky and my aunt might talk for a minute or so and she can relax and enjoy the smoke. But often her puff is interrupted as my aunt asks a quick question that demands a quick response. In these cases, Mom has become an expert, like most Newfoundland women, at speaking while inhaling. "Yahm. Yahm"—the breathy word for agreement that Mom and so many others say when they just can't wait long enough to breathe to start talking.

She is on the same beige phone plugged in under the cupboards at the L of the counter. Same phone, in the exact same spot on the wall, that's been there for as long as I can remember. Same curly cord stretching out from the same faded mouthpiece with the grey plastic peeking out from under the retreating beige, worn away by a couple of decades of chatter, gossip, whispers to boyfriends and girlfriends, screams at bill collectors, good news and bad.

It is the same phone that had practically the same phone number as a photo printing store in St. John's called Cambell's. One digit was different. That phone rang so often with people asking if this was "the picture place" that we started saying, "Yes, of course this is Cambell's."

Some poor frigger on the other end: "Are my pictures back from developing?"

Terribly, we'd carry on with the ruse. "Yes ... Mr. ... Smith? Yes, they are here. Drop down anytime. We stay open till 2 a.m. every night of the week. Just bang on the door really loud if the gate is closed on Water Street."

One time, home alone, I answered a call from a gent looking for his photos. "Yes, sir, your photos are here, but we'll have to hold them for questioning."

Poor confused frigger on the other end: "Why, what's the problem?"

"Well sir, these photos show a lady in very little clothing with a man almost as undressed. Is that you, sir?"

Poor angry frigger coming unglued: "What! Jesus Christ, no, that's not me! I'll be down to the shop in a minute, though, and I'll find out who the bastard is!"

With some regret, I offer the owners and patrons of Cambell's a silent apology as I watch Mom now on that same phone speaking into the same faded mouthpiece.

Same phone. Same corner. Same Mom. Perfect.

"Yes, the children are all doing so grand, and how nice is it to have them all home now," Mom repeats to my aunt on the other end of the line and seems to be answering specific questions about each of the kids. "Yes, Michelle is just about to graduate with the top honours in Grade 12 and got accepted in to music school. She's gonna do two degrees now, one in music and an education degree as well. Yes, and honey, Kim got her second degree in occupational therapy from Dalhousie. And Bernie is all graduated with civil engineering degree, near the top of his class, and is going to get his MBA next, in Montreal."

Mom pauses. The silence raises my eyebrow. Finally she says, "Oh, yes. Alan is here." She pauses again for what feels like a long time but may just be seconds, takes a draw and inhale-speaks. "Yahm yahm, you knows what he's like, honey. Playing in the band, happy as anything."

When the phone call ends, Mom takes a second to survey the stove and calls everyone to the table, "before it all gets cold." As the plates and second plates of potatoes and gravy are being wiped clean with thick warm slices of white bread, the conversation quickly turns to what everyone is at. Kim, professional and organized as ever, tells of a method she's devised to more efficiently document and report patient visits at her clinic, or something like that. Bernie tells of a paving company that tried unsuccessfully to dupe him, the junior onsite engineer, by using the wrong mixture and width of pavement on a job he was overseeing, or something like that. Michelle, still my baby sister in her late teens, tells of the trouble she's having deciding which of the musicals she will do in the spring, as three different producers want her to play the lead, or something like that.

In the past I would have been as talkative as them, but on this day, having been away for four-fifths of the last year, I just want to listen to them all. The chatter is as reassuring as Mom's cooking.

"What a gang," I said to no one in particular as I reached for the last heel of bread.

"You're some quiet." Mom probably knew I was happy to listen but figured I'd been granted enough reprieve. "Where were you this last trip?"

"Oh, we played a festival in Saint John and then up to a Legion hall in Miramichi and then a school thing in Rothesay."

Dad did not look up from his plate. "So mostly there by Halifax, like."

My sister said, "No, Dad, that's all New Brunswick." Kim knows the Atlantic area very well, having schooled there for so long.

"Yeah, but pretty close, like."

As noted, Kim is a stickler for the details. "Well, about four hundred kilometres away. So about as close as Grand Falls."

"Yeah, that's right." As Dad marries carrot and turnip on his fork, we can't tell if he has learned anything or not from this conversation. He does not look up from the potatoes and gravy, either way.

"Now, who did you see that you knows?" Mom is eating like a bird, or perhaps just sensibly, compared to the rest of us. "Did you see any of Roger's crowd?" She asks with honest curiosity, and all the kids know she wants the answer to be yes more than anything at this moment.

"Who's Roger?" I ask.

"You knows Roger, honey, your second or third cousin. Uncle Jerry's crowd that were home a couple summers ago down to Petty Harbour Day . . . Buddy with the odd-looking baseball hat on."

My siblings and I try not to give each other a knowing glance, but we cannot help it. This is where Mom will try to convince us we remember a distant family member we may or may not have met in passing anywhere from very recently to many years ago. She continues, determined, if not desperate to convince me I might very well have bumped into my third cousin who I may have met one time and will no doubt recall because he had a strange hat.

"I don't think I would know him, Mom." I don't want to totally dismiss her, though, so I ask, "Where does he live?"

She lays down her fork and rubs her forehead. "Oh, I don't know for sure, honey. Somewhere there near Halifax, I suppose. What's it called, Tom?"

"Up on the mainland somewhere. That's all I knows." Dad still does not look up from the potatoes and gravy.

And so it went for that and many happy homecoming suppers to my Petty Harbour home. There were always curious questions about the places I'd seen, and I would have to report on whether there really was a shipyard in Yarmouth, and if you could really drive uphill at Magnetic Hill.

Dad, once a semi-professional musician himself, would ask questions about the gigs with more watchfulness than most, though he worked hard to hide how proud he was of my good fortune by turning the conversation back to himself.

"Where were ye all this trip?" Dad would still not look up from his plate of potatoes and gravy.

"Oh, we played the Lower Deck in Halifax."

"Yes, I heard of that place. Stan Rogers used to play there. Me and Ronnie knows a good few Stan Rogers tunes."

Or, "Where did you play last week, my son?"

"It was so awesome, Dad. We got to play with the Chieftains at a recording studio in Halifax." Surely this one would expose a chink in his armour. Surely he would throw his hands in the air and shout, "What!? The Chieftains! Jaysus, my son, that's amazing!"

But he was not to be swayed. "Yes, b'y, the Chieftains. They played a few good ones. We used to play them too. Me and your uncles Ronnie and Leonard and Jimmy, on *All Around the Circle* on TV. Great old Irish songs, b'y. I tell you, they loved us on *All Around the Circle*."

It became a near ritual. Like reciting the mass.

Dad: "Where were you this trip?"

Me: "I played Carnegie Hall with Bob Dylan and Elvis."

Dad: "Yes, b'y, me and Ronnie and them played a few halls too. St. George's hall over on the South Side, and Witless Bay hall dozens of times, sure. I tell you, they loved us at the Witless Bay hall."

Me: "Right."

Through it all, I always knew my brother and sisters and Mom and Dad were happy that I was out doing what I loved. My parents tried their very best to forget I had left a really good government job at the Newfoundland Museum to start Great Big Sea; a government job that would be paying me almost forty thousand by my mid-twenties.

There was no clearer evidence of their desire for me to have some kind of fallback plan than one supper visit when my sisters giggled and told Mom and Dad I had a new girlfriend.

"Yes, b'y." Dad still did not look up from his potatoes and gravy.

"Oh my, honey!" Mom was excited. "Where did you meet her?"

I explained that I'd been helping my bandmate Séan look for an apartment, and at a well-kept old house in downtown St. John's a beautiful gal showed us the second-floor apartment that was for rent. I was desperate to say something really cool, and I came up with "Do you live here, too?"

"Brilliant." My sister Kim was having a great laugh.

"What a ladies man!" Sister Michelle was not going to let Kim have all the fun.

"Shush, ye two!" Mom wanted to hear all the details.

I went on to tell how the beautiful gal told me her name was Joanne and she lived in the main-floor apartment.

"Oh," I said to her, "you look after the place for a break on the rent or whatever. That's cool. The owner must love to have you."

My sisters bust out laughing. "You dick!" they said in unison, knowing the whole story.

"Shush, I said, the two of ye!" Mom flicked a dish cloth at them like a beach towel.

I continued to tell of how Joanne replied in the most kind and unassuming voice, "Oh, no. You're a bit confused. I *am* the owner of this house. I used the grant portion of my student loan for a down payment, then paid back the loan, and the rent from the other two apartments pays the mortgage and taxes, and a little bit more." Then she pushed her perfectly permed black hair behind her ear and smiled. "I figure, why rent a house when you can own it and collect rent from others?" I was in love with her before she showed Séan the bathroom.

I almost took a knee right there and then. (Truth be told, it would take me a few more years to take a knee, but when I did, she said yes. The Fairest of Them All is my wife and we have a wonderful son, Henry. I can hear them both upstairs as I type. I am the luckiest person I know.)

Mom was over the moon. "My God, honey! You got to bring her out so we can meet her! She sounds delightful. Pretty, and smart, and got her own house and everything. What does she do for a living?"

Michelle answered before I could. "That's the best part, Mom. She's already got a big job, don't she, Kim?"

Kim jumped right in. "Yes, she got the biggest kind of job with the Department of Fisheries. She's a naval architect."

The sound of a fork hitting a plate broke the excitement. We all turned to see Dad finally looking up from his plate. His head tilted ever slightly to one side like a dog trying to decipher its master's words.

"She's a what?" he deadpanned.

"She's a naval architect." Kim sounded even more impressed the second time around.

I could see the wheels turning in his head. "Son left good-paying government job . . . met a girl with her own house and a big government job . . . and is a naval friggin' architect." I swear I could see him calculating the whole equation in his mind, formulating his response, and I swear I could see the moment he came to it. Both his eyebrows raised like a mad scientist who'd just solved a long-aching problem. He turned to me as a man with the most sound and sage advice ever delivered. And when he spoke, he spoke with complete certainty.

"Knock her up."

QUEBEC

"You are a bunch of c—t." Our very Québécois host, Jean, despite his odd use of the singular, was clearly referring to Séan and me. "You Newfoundlander! You are all c—t. You two are c—t. And all your friend are c—t."

For the past hour or so I had been drinking what looked to be the world's largest Labatt Cinquante. I didn't think I'd ever get to the end of it. They seemed to only sell extra-large bottles of beer and heavy red wine by the full bottle not by the glass at this very sovereigntist pub in Quebec City. After we'd played a gig at le Festival d'été, the premier music festival in Quebec, Séan and I had been led here by Jean, the ringleader of the unofficial host band. We sat back to back astride a long, narrow bench pulled up to a worn wooden table. Our backs were touching, leaning against each other every now and again, but we were having completely different conversations. If Séan had had an ear to mine he would have heard me chatting with a gang of local musicians about Newfoundland's only French community, the Port au Port

Peninsula. But instead it was I who caught snippets of his conversation and more specifically of Séan asking Jean why he was calling us all a bunch of c—t. I had to stop my chat and turn my attention to his.

It was our first-ever visit to Quebec City, and within minutes of driving into the town I had fallen in love with it. It had a sense of place entirely its own, as if I had entered a different country altogether. People didn't eat the same food at the same times of day or wear the same kind of clothing or eyeglasses. Even the way they wore their scarves was cooler than anything I'd ever seen before. As soon as I could, I wandered through the walled city. It was as if the place was a massive Cabot Tower with the heart of downtown inside it. Unlike at home, where St. John's folks could look up high upon the relatively tiny stone structure atop Signal Hill, here the city itself lived and breathed within the hold of the castle.

I'd heard rumours that Quebec City was full of people who wanted to separate from Canada. As a kid on the wharf in Petty Harbour, I'd eavesdropped on conversations the fishermen would have about Quebec. They'd often complain that the Quebec fishermen got a far better deal from the federal government, and, as Larry would say while gutting fish, "us Newfoundlanders are getting nothing." John would jump right in: "Yes, and 'cause they got all the seats, see, and we only got five or six. No odds if the crowd in Ottawa pisses us off. We're not worth nothin' to them." Larry would agree. "Yes, though I don't know what good them seats are to them if half of them are a bunch of separatists."

Within an hour of this first visit in the mid-nineties, I could tell that the rumours I'd heard on the wharf were true. The vast majority of the people I spoke to wore Quebec nationalist symbols on their coats. Separatist signs were plastered everywhere.

Every third or fourth person at the festival site wore some kind of Quebec nationalist T-shirt.

From the news, I knew many Canadians were upset by the very notion of the Quebec separatist movement. From the darkest days of the late sixties to the recent Quebec referendum, the mere mention of Quebec's discord with the government of Canada gave many folks the shivers. I suppose I was less threatened by it all because I'd grown up with talk that was very similar.

Ever since the Confederation vote was tallied at a narrow 51–49 margin in favour of joining Canada, a strain of Newfoundlanders has been crying foul. Many ironies and odd circumstances of history have led many to all-out conspiracy theories about a rigged vote. The fact that the ballots had been shipped away and hidden in England has many Newfoundland republicans pacing the halls to this day. The fact that we were joining a country whose day of celebration is July first, which in Newfoundland was a long-established day of sombre remembrance of our war heroes, caused a near-multiple-personality condition. And what to make of the fact that Newfoundland was set to join Canada on April Fools' Day? What to make of how they rushed to sign the deal to join Canada near midnight on March thirty-first to avoid that historical joke. And yet diehard republican Newfoundlanders cannot help but lift an eyebrow when April first comes around, and we note the day we swore in our first provincial premier.

I had participated in heated, often drunken debates at university about a return to an independent Newfoundland. But I knew where I belonged, so a fleur-de-lys flag or *Québec Libre* T-shirt was not about to send me running for the hills. Though I did wonder if this would make for a crowd of unwelcoming people, I found nothing of the sort. Especially around festival time, it seemed all arms and doors were open to everyone. And that was good enough for me.

Through the open doors of le Festival d'été in Quebec City, the language barrier seemed to disappear in songs. All hands were equally eager to sing in French or English or, I suspect, any other language. It made me wonder why the province of Quebec was so uncharted by most Canadian bands. It all felt so accessible and welcoming that day. Why, I wondered, weren't there more such opportunities.

As I type here today, some twenty years after I first played Quebec, I wonder the same thing.

The biggest thing I can tell you about Quebec is that I know very little about Quebec. For a fella who has travelled in Canada as much as me, it is incredible how little of Quebec I have experienced. I have been to the Montreal area many times and Quebec City about a half-dozen times. I did a festival gig across the water from Bathurst, New Brunswick, and a corporate gig in Mont-Tremblant, and I spent a wacky few days in the biggest log cabin in the world near Montebello shooting a TV special. To some, that might sound like a wealth of experience in any province, but consider that I have been to practically every Canadian town outside of Quebec with more than twenty-five thousand people. A quick look at the 2011 census tells me I have played practically every one of those towns in Ontario. Yet there are cities of hundreds of thousands in Quebec that I have never played.

Laval has almost half a million people, and I've never even been there. Gatineau has a quarter of a million people and I've never played a concert there. I have never been to Sherbrooke, Trois-Rivières, or Chicoutimi, all of which are big cities by my standards. Châteaugay, Drummondville, Saint-Jérôme, and Granby all have more than fifty thousand, and I couldn't point to a couple of them on the map. There are over a dozen other cities in Quebec with more than twenty-five thousand people. I've been to none of them.

I wish it wasn't so, and it amazes me that this is even possible. You'd think it would be impossible for a band from Atlantic Canada that has played so often in Ontario to have played so little in Quebec. You've got to drive right through one to get to the other. I know many more major Canadian acts that have played all over Canada except Quebec. A band from Halifax is more likely to play Vancouver before most of Quebec. That's like a band from New York playing Anchorage before Boston. It remains a mystery to me.

I think back to the map of Canada I drew as a kid. It is amazing to me that if you asked me to fill in the same map now, it would look much the same as it did about forty years ago. I would only add one other city to the Quebec section. My map would still be dominated by Montreal, and it remains one of my favourite places in the world.

I was just old enough to understand and enjoy hockey on TV when the Montreal Canadiens cemented their legacy as a dynasty unrivalled in professional sports. From the time I was seven until I was ten, the Habs won four Stanley Cups in a row, and just about every Saturday I got to watch them on *Hockey Night in Canada*. I watched Ken Dryden make saves and Guy Lafleur score goals, but after a while, I realized I was watching the people in the stands just as much. When the TV coverage switched to city and crowd scenes outside the rink, and most everyone else in the room went for their chips, I was transfixed.

I loved the way the people dressed up for the games, the men in suits and ties and long overcoats, the ladies in dresses and makeup and hairdos. And everyone smoked, including the players. The shots of the city on winter nights were like quick glances of another world. The big cross on the hill. The trains zipping around the city. Old Montreal with horse-drawn carriages and cobblestone streets where they ate some kind of doughnut-shaped bread called a bagel and put gravy and cheese on their chips. If you had asked me as a ten-year-old where in the world I most wanted to go, I would have said Montreal to watch a Canadiens game at the Forum. I would have easily picked it over a beach vacation or a trip to the greatest amusement park on earth—and I still would.

I could not wait to finally set foot in the Narnia of my childhood. I expected there might be French food, like croissants and coffee, and even Québécois fare like poutine, but I was not prepared for the world of food available in that city. I suppose I was just not aware of how international a city Montreal is, and in turn, of how many international communities have brought with them the best of their kitchens. I sampled all I could. So many of my food firsts happened in Montreal. I had my first Jewish bagel at St-Viateur. Smoked meat sandwiches at a place called Ben's almost convinced me to move. I found shish tawook from a restaurant, not a lady, called Sarah, to be an incredible late-night feed. Caprese salad, I discovered at Pizzeria Napoletana, was salad with no lettuce in it. Honest to God. And it was there I had my very first espresso, which kick-started a love affair and addiction that runs to this day.

In Montreal I learned that "appetizer" was a category of food, and not a singular thing that we got at Christmastime when aunts and uncles came over. "Perhaps I'll make some appetizers," Mom would say, then she'd open three cans of Vienna sausages, cut them in half, and slide them onto toothpicks. She'd cube up "hard" cheese, which I would come to learn was cheddar, and slide it on the toothpick behind the sausage. The final ingredient in "appetizers" was a pickled small white onion. If she wanted to be really fancy, she would cut a large orange or grapefruit in half and place it flat side down on a plate. She'd poke the "appetizers" in the dome of the fruit and display it as proudly as Martha Stewart would a soufflé.

Montreal also had Indian, Chinese, Japanese, and other Asian restaurants. I regularly start a racket with friends from London, England, or Sydney, Australia, or even New York, when I defend my position that Montreal is the best food city in the world. It offers the most variety for any budget.

On my first couple of days in Montreal chasing food delights around the city, I became aware of something about Newfoundland, and St. John's in particular, that I had not fully appreciated before. We have almost no ethnic food variety. And that's because we have almost no ethnic variety. St. John's had no taco restaurant because we don't really have any Mexicans. Surely there's a half-dozen somewhere, but there is no discernible visible minority group of Latin American people. You can't get a great bowl of spaghetti because we don't have any Italians. No bratwurst because we have practically no Germans. No perogies because we have no Ukrainians. You get the picture.

In the 1996 census, done shortly after my first visit to Montreal, the total population of Newfoundland was 574,446. Of this number, 538,695 spoke English as a first language. Our largest visible minority was people of Chinese descent, with a population of a few hundred.

In Montreal I had my first real taste of Canada's famous multiculturalism, and realized just how homogeneously settled Newfoundland was. So homogeneously settled that the arrival of folks from other ethnic backgrounds causes a most welcome stir and in some cases has literally become the stuff of legends.

There are dozens of tales of folks who came to be stuck on the island, shipwrecked or otherwise. Many of these stranded souls would recall that the hospitality of Newfoundlanders towards people of all races and creeds and colours had changed their world view.

African American Lanier Phillips was born in the racially segregated world of Lithonia, Georgia, in 1923. As a young man he witnessed and suffered through the racism and violence of the Ku Klux Klan. He once spoke at a gathering I was lucky enough to attend, and even as an elderly man he trembled remembering the horrors he had seen.

As a teenager he joined the navy to escape the South, but found himself in a world every bit as racist as the one he had left behind. Black men in the navy were limited to lower ranks, and opportunities for advancement were virtually non-existent.

In February 1942, during the coldest days of winter, Lanier was aboard USS *Truxtun* when a storm struck hard near the Burin Peninsula of Newfoundland. The *Truxtun* and USS *Pollux* were driven onto the rocks in Chambers Cove, not far from the small fishing village of St. Lawrence. Many men died, but Lanier, soaked with oil from the ships, was among those who fought through the icy sea water to the steep banks of Newfoundland.

Local fishermen and miners ran to the wreckage and helped lift the sailors up the cliffs and away from certain death. "I was covered in oil, and freezing to sure death, but I knew I had to make it to that beach," Lanier told me. "When I got there I thought there's no way I can climb up that hill that stood before me. I was too exhausted. I must have collapsed and was minutes from freezing when my eyes opened to a white man's face. He was helping me up the hill and encouraging me to climb with him or die on this beach. That man helped me, a black man from the South, just the same as he helped everyone else. If it had been in Georgia, a white man would have kicked me out of the way. I'd never seen anything like it."

Lanier and the others made it up the hill and were quickly taken inside to be warmed and washed clean by the local women. Lanier's eyes opened wider and his gestures broadened as he remembered. "Now, Alan, you've got to understand, I was warned from a very young age not to so much as look at a white woman or I'd be hanged on the spot. And here I was, naked, with two white women washing me and whispering to me that everything was going to be okay."

This is where this story, like many stories in Newfoundland, sounds fantastical, but is 100 per cent true. From the man himself, "The ladies were washing all the men who'd been covered in oil. They would not stop till every one of them was back to their white flesh. The lady stood over me and said to the other, 'My dear, I'm having some trouble getting the tar off this fella. I've scrubbed and scrubbed and he's still black.' I looked up and said, 'Ma'am, that's not the oil. That's the colour of my skin.' I thought for sure I would be killed for speaking to a white lady directly, but then she took me to her house and put me in her bed she'd warmed with stones from the fire. I lay there wondering if I had died and gone to heaven." He told me he knew there and then that all people could be and should be treated equally. He would go on to become a civil rights leader in the U.S. and joined Dr. Martin Luther King on more than one occasion. He smashed the colour barrier and became the first-ever African American sonar technician in the U.S. Navy.

If I could say one thing about our early gigs in Montreal and Quebec City, it would be that despite our many differences,

Newfoundlanders and Quebecers have at least two things in common. They both love to celebrate and they both love to sing. If you ask a Quebec audience to sing along, you better be ready for a response, because it is coming hard.

Newfoundlanders and Quebecers have a shared history of being outsiders in Canada, and I wish I could tell you our shared history has made Newfoundland–Quebec relations more harmonious, yet nothing could be further from the truth. The battles over the boundary between the two provinces were fierce. There's hardly a Newfoundlander alive who does not resent the Churchill Falls hydro deal, wherein Quebec still pays 1950s prices for power produced in Newfoundland and Labrador. Newfoundland was one of the last holdouts refusing to sign the Quebec-friendly Meech Lake Accord just a few years back and many Quebecers were not happy about our holding out. Quebec and Newfoundland and Labrador might be seen as step-brothers, at best reluctant family members brought together by a marriage neither wanted very much in the first place.

That night in Quebec City, after our enthusiastically received festival gig, and over music, wine, and giant Cinquantes, the conversation between Séan and Jean had turned to the recent and distant history of those relations.

"You are a bunch of c—t. You are c—t. And all your friend are c—t."

Séan, as always cool as a cucumber: "Why would you say that?"

"You come 'ere wit' your friendly smile, your French songs de Terre-Neuve, and you h'act like a friend to Quebec. But you are no friend to Quebec."

"Why do you say that?" Séan persisted.

"Because you f—k us with the Meech Lake. You f—k us bad," Jean said, a finger pointing now.

The entire table hushed. Like someone had spoken a forbidden phrase. Like something had been said that could not be taken back. A silence that felt like forever hung over the whole bar as Séan took a long drag on a cigarette. He flicked the ash into an ashtray.

"Yeah, but you guys f—ked us with Churchill Falls."

Now the hush in the room turned into a gasp.

Jean's eyes widened. "Churchill Fall?" he asked, not as if he needed Séan to repeat it but more like he *dared* Séan to repeat it. Then his face changed in an instant. He let out a huge laugh as he raised his Cinquante to the others around the room. "Ah, yes. Churchill Fall. Dat was a good one."

And we all went back to singing and drinking together.

LANGUAGE

fter I returned from Quebec, having had my first experience with a legitimate language barrier, I was more
aware than ever of the colourful Newfoundland tongue.
And I could see for the first time just how confusing it might be to
English speakers from elsewhere and how nearly indecipherable
it was to folks who speak English as a second language.

I'd first considered our vocabulary and dialect as potentially
difficult to decipher by those more accustomed to Hollywood
American or the Queen's English when I was in my mid-teens
and a tour guide at the Newfoundland Museum. This was the first
place I ever had to temper my local dialect if I was going to keep
my job and have tourists understand a single sentence that came
out of my mouth. If a visitor from the mainland asked if we had a
restroom, it would do none of us any good if I responded in my
full Petty Harbour tongue. For clarity I'll try to write phoneti-
cally, and you should imagine the sentence coming about twice as
fast as you might think possible.

"Yaum, we got two tilets here, over dere, luh."

I tried to standardize my dialect a bit, but I did not always get it right. I can recall a few tourists standing with blank faces at the museum desk waiting for me to speak to them in a language they understood. I knew there was a group of academics coming to view the military history display on the third floor. When they arrived I said, "What are ye at? I s'pose ye wants to see the guns and 'dat? Yeah, wouldn't blame ye one bit, 'cause there's all kind of wicked stuff on the t'ird floor. Dart up the stairs or take the elevators if ye wants."

Mine is a common Irish-influenced dialect spoken on the Southern Shore of the Avalon Peninsula around Petty Harbour, Bay Bulls, and Witless Bay. But there are dozens, if not hundreds, of other dialects around the island. There are entire books and university courses dedicated to the complex mélange of histories and influences that have formed the various ways of speaking the same language in one province.

I'll name just a few of those various ways.

Many dialects in Newfoundland have efficiently simplified the conjugation of most verbs. Instead of the foolishly complicated "I run, you run, he, she, it runs" kind of thing, many Newfoundlanders agree on "I runs, you runs, we all runs."

Common dialects in Newfoundland add *h*'s to words starting with a vowel and remove the *h* when it begins a word. *Apple* becomes *h'apple* and *have* becomes *'ave*. So "H'are you 'ungry? Why don't you 'ave a h'apple?" I could not believe when the local hardware store in Arnold's Cove near my summer cabin got bought out by the national chain Home Hardware. If you called and just about anyone answered the phone, you would hear, "'Ome 'ardware, H'Arnolds Cove." You couldn't make this stuff up.

Oh, I could go on forever about *th* pronounced mostly like *d* and *ing* endings that sound like *in* and the complete mystery of the word *luh*, which I think means "there" and others think means "look" but no one is totally sure. "Look, dats him walkin' dere, luh."

An oddity that I never heard as a kid in Petty Harbour but have grown to love the most is the use of the word *n*, pronounced "en" as at the end of *written*. In parts of Newfoundland, this word can mean many things. Often it can mean "him." So instead of hearing "Oh she loves him," you'd hear "Oh she loves'n." But it can also mean "it," as in "The mail's in the box, go get'n, willya?"

Where Americans might say "buddy," and Australians might say "mate," folks from some parts of Newfoundland say "b'y" a lot, as in "Hey, b'y, are we gonna get a storm?" Other folks from up the shore might say "old man," as in "Jesus, old man, you knows we're going to get a storm." Still others might add a "buddy, my son," said quickly as in "Buddymussun, the storm is gonna be wicked."

There are so many tweaks and turns that the language can become an awesome maze, especially when some of the above elements are combined. As a teenager, I was in the Marystown area when, as young teens do, I got into a scrap with a local around my age. He turned to me and said, "Buddymussun, I'm gonna pick up a rock and 'it ya right in da 'ead with'n. Yes, h'old man, I gonna split ya h'open if you don't shag off."

And then there is the nearly impossible to describe use of the phrase *after doing*, which I would say most often means "just done." "Now look what I'm after doing." Imagine a Spanish person who'd been studying English words and tenses trying to figure out the sentence "Now look what I'm after doing." Not to mention the odd use of negatives to mean positives in some parts of Newfoundland. My friend was an employment counsellor in the Clarenville area when a recently laid-off fish plant worker came in looking for work. He stood in the doorway looking eager to get at something and asked, "I don't s'pose you don't know no one who don't want nothing done, do ya?" Add to that the odd use of negatives and the odder use of the word "perhaps," which actually means "definitely," as in "Perhaps I won't be going to the dance tonight and having a few drinks while I'm up 'dere! Yes, b'y, perhaps I won't!" Good luck explaining that to the exchange student from Copenhagen.

Hospitable as we are, I think it is fair to say some of us Newfoundlanders have a hard time appreciating how other people might hear our language. This, I suspect, is because we have so little experience with . . . well, with other people.

My sister Kim has worked in health care in Newfoundland for her entire career. She tells the tale of how she had an intern from Ontario named Sheila working with her one summer and assigned her the task of doing a few preliminary interviews with patients as they arrived.

It was all going well and four or five patients came and went without a hitch. Then young Sheila came into Kim's office quite flustered, and my super-professional sister asked what the problem could be.

"Well, I've got this gentleman in there and I can't figure out what's wrong with him."

"What did he say when you asked him?"

Sheila was getting more upset. "Well, that's just it. I don't really understand what he means. He says he's looking for body parts or a shoulder or something. Should I call the psychiatric nurse?"

Kim figured she'd better check things out for herself. She walked into the examining room to find Mr. Hunt, a man in his mid-seventies. One glance at his hands and she rightly assumed he had been a fisherman his whole life. According to his chart he was healthy as a horse and almost as big and strong.

"Mr. Hunt," she said a bit louder than she needed to, "what seems to be the trouble?"

"Well, my love, I can't mind a single time with any kind of pain anywhere at all, hey. But I must say, these past few weeks, I finds me arm. I especially finds it wicked in the damp, hey."

Kim nodded and turned to Shelia, wondering what the confusion might be. "He finds his arm."

With Sheila's continued look of bewilderment, a look that said "these people are all crazy," Kim realized that something was lost in translation.

"Oh. He finds his arm. As in he finds his arm to be sore." She turned back to Mr. Hunt. "You finds it the most in the cold wet weather, Mr. Hunt?"

"Yes, my dear, I hardly finds it at all in the sunshine."

Kim turned back to Sheila. "Pretty sure he has arthritis in his elbow. Do an X-ray and send him for an arthritis test."

I believe the intern returned to the mainland shortly afterwards.

ONTARIO 1

"We ran out of beer." Keith, the head bartender at the legendary Horseshoe Tavern in Toronto, was standing in the doorway of the grungy dressing room in the basement.

There was space for just three people to sit on the bench attached to the wall, so I was leaning on the door frame and was the only one who heard him speak.

"What do you mean? The bar is going well? Lotta drinkers up there, for sure."

"No, man. Seriously, we ran out of beer during your first set. Hopefully the trucks will be done reloading before you guys go back on. Just wanted to let you know in case you were wondering why we were doing a beer delivery during your set."

Great Big Sea was playing one of its first real headline concerts in Toronto. After a few bar gigs on the Danforth and a slot on a multi-band bill at a show bar on Queen Street, we had landed a gig at the Horseshoe Tavern. The Horseshoe is the stepping stone to every other gig in Toronto, and it might even be fair to say the stepping stone to a real place in the Canadian music business. In the mid-nineties, when record companies still had some money and employees, their A & R (Artists and Repertoire) people all but camped at the Horseshoe to see who was up-and-coming. A good night there was worth ten anywhere else.

I thought I knew a lot about Southern Ontario by the time I hit my early twenties. And compared to the other provinces, I probably did. I figured I knew a bunch about Toronto and Ottawa, as they were both on TV so much and both had a professional sports team I cheered for at one point or another, in the Blue Jays and the Rough Riders. I could even tell you a few other towns that were close by, like Cambridge, where a bunch of Newfoundlanders had moved to work in auto plants and factories, and Kingston, where there was a big university and an even bigger prison, I thought. Ontario is Newfoundland's most popular and successful sibling. The country's favourite kid. The star of the family who the others are sometimes jealous of but are really quite proud of and secretly love.

I had a few cousins from each side of the family who left Petty Harbour or Marystown to work in the Greater Toronto Area. Some of the older guard in the family were convinced these kids would be killed or return as drug addicts if they spent too much time "up there." I thought this unlikely, but when a few of them returned with mainlander accents, I began to wonder if they might have been messed with somehow.

I knew a couple of other things—that there was a place north of Toronto where mainlanders had cabins on lakes that they called cottages for some reason. And finally, that Windsor,

Ontario, was close to Detroit, as *Hockey Night in Canada* regularly showed both cities and the river in between when the Red Wings played.

My sister Kim had worked for a while in a hospital in St. Thomas, Ontario, but could never seem to convince anyone around home that she'd not been working in Toronto.

"How's it going up in Chronto?" my aunt would ask Kim when she was home for a holiday.

Kim, ever professional and precise, would answer, "Oh, the hospital is south of London, Ontario, actually. About halfway between Hamilton and Detroit."

My aunt would look confused but smile and nod. "Right. So Chronto, really."

I had no idea that just a few years later, Bob, Séan, Darrell, and I would be steering a rented station wagon through the maze of transport trucks heading into Canada's biggest urban centre. And we were freaked completely out. There has never been a fish so far out of water as a fella from the twisty narrow paths of Petty Harbour flopping around on the massive highways of Southern Ontario. The traffic on the infamous 401 is enough to make a Newfoundlander turn around and drive home. By the time Great Big Sea hit the road, I had spent nearly every waking hour of my life on the Southern Shore or in St. John's. I had never seen a highway bigger than four lanes. Now, eight lanes of highway went in each direction. "Miss an exit and we're screwed, b'ys, so keep your eyes open." Up in the passenger seat, Bob would be spinning the map in his hands like a steering wheel, trying to read the tiny print. At times every lane was bumper to bumper with every vehicle going 130 kilometres an hour. Other times the traffic slowed to a stop, the highway becoming a parking lot sixteen lanes wide.

On our first few days in the Toronto area, I became aware of so many things I'd never even heard of. I was shocked, for example, that Toronto has a beach. A big one, with people playing volleyball and lying under umbrellas in sand and rollerblading along a paved recreation trail that seemed to never end. The beach ran along a lake so big that it looked more like a bay than any lake in Newfoundland. "Is it still a lake if you can't see the other side of it?" I asked in the van. "They don't call them the Great Lakes for nothing," someone replied, but I did not turn my head to see who. I was too busy staring at so many things I'd not expected to see. All along the beach and boardwalk were some posh houses, but on the streets behind those were quite modest family homes on small streets not unlike many parts of St. John's. I cannot tell you how surprised I was to see this. In all my imaginings of the city of Toronto, I pictured skyscrapers, apartment buildings, sports stadiums, and CN Towers, and I was prepared to see all of those things. I'd never once thought that Toronto might have houses in it.

The sidewalks downtown were busier than the highways leading into the city. When I lived in St. John's, I walked from my frat house to just about everywhere else I had to go. I walked in one direction to Memorial University, and another to downtown to work at the museum or go to gigs on George Street. I honestly had no memory of ever paying attention to any traffic signals during those walks. I just watched for cars and made my way sensibly enough. But here in Toronto, you were taking your life into your hands if you did not wait for the white walking fella. And when he finally lit up, you could lift your feet and be carried across by the mass of people going from one side to the other.

Our first gig in Toronto, at Quinn's on the Danforth, was around St. Patrick's Day. The half-filled room was mostly occupied by friends my cousin Jamie had brought along and, you guessed it, a few buddies of Darrell's. Not a raging hit, but a start, I figured, and at least I'd finally be able tell Mom that I saw someone that I knows.

We had been doing a few opening sets and festival dates around Southern Ontario early that summer, and Louis, then our agent and later our manager, figured we should take a leap of faith and book the Horseshoe for a headline set. It would be a huge step if it sold well and a confirmation that we were nothing but a good pub band if it didn't. But he believed we could do the business, and we agreed to go for it.

There would have been some advance sales, but back then it was tough to get accurate ticket counts, and we were biting our nails as the day approached. I remember walking from the SkyDome Hotel to the sound check early in the afternoon. We had landed some posh rooms at the hotel, which overlooked the domed sports field. We most certainly could not have afforded to pay the going rate for any of these rooms, the cheapest of which would have been several hundreds of dollars when our budget was tens of dollars.

Again, true to form, Darrell had a buddy, a fella he'd gone to school with or something who had recently landed a job as the head concierge at the hotel. Doug could get us the staff rate for the cheapest rooms in the hotel, which amounted to about $75, and then he could upgrade us to any available room in the hotel. So here we were, on a shoestring budget, staying in hotel rooms overlooking the World Series–winning Toronto Blue Jays.

We held many meetings with agents and label representatives and college buyers while watching a sporting event in digs that our guests assumed we were successful enough to pay for. It was worth the cash to have a meeting at the SkyDome restaurant and seat our guests facing the elevators and watch their faces as famous musicians, actors, and sports personalities walked through the lobby. The college buyers were especially impressed by this set-up, and I'm sure went back to their bosses with descriptions of what a big deal we were and assurances that our asking fee was not exorbitant at all.

Rubbing shoulders with the rich and famous made us feel all right too. We often stood in the lobby as sports celebrities and famous actors and politicians checked in and out. Bobby Orr walked past me and Bob in the lobby once, and to our astonishment winked and said, "Hey, fellas. Great day out there." I quite nearly wet my drawers.

"It's a long way from the Inglis House, Bob," I said with a grin.

"Yep. Hopefully a long way back, too." Bob winked for good luck.

Late one night Darrell and I wandered back to the hotel after some post-gig frolicking. We went directly to the elevators, and just as the doors were about to shut, a huge hand slipped in and forced them back open. A mountain of a man in black boots, black pants, and a high black turtleneck stretched over his muscle-bound chest stood before us.

"You fellas mind stepping out, please?" His voice had an urgency that was hard to ignore.

"Sorry?" I asked, because I honestly wasn't sure what was happening and stood on my tiptoes to look over his shoulder.

Behind him hovered two other people that matched his description, walkie-talkies in hand, surveying the empty lobby as if they were sweeping the airport for bombs. There, behind those two, was a tall, good-looking fella who appeared somewhat embarrassed that his team was going through this routine for no apparent reason. I instantly recognized him as one of the singers from New Kids on the Block, who was in town promoting a solo recording, I thought. We'd seen throngs of fans in a few places around town, but not here, not now.

The big gent looked us both up and down and repeated, "Sorry, you fellas mind stepping out, please?"

From where he stood in the elevator, Darrell could not see any of the others in the entourage and politely asked, "Why?"

The big gent was getting impatient, and repeated a third time, "You fellas mind stepping out, please? We need this elevator for Jordan."

Darrell quite reasonably asked, "The whole country?"

The big fella was not impressed, so I grabbed Darrell by the sleeve and led him out to the lobby, barely able to stand I was laughing so hard.

Jordan Knight, a man who could buy and sell us a thousand times over, looked humiliated as he shrugged his shoulders. "Sorry about this, guys. You want to ride along? It's cool."

"We haven't cleared these guys, Jordan. Are you sure?" The big fella spoke with a concern that seemed equally professional and ludicrous. Before Jordan could respond, I figured I should let him off the hook.

"Nah, do what you gotta do, man."

Jordan Knight reached between two security guards and shook my hand and said, "Sorry, man. Thank you."

That night I lay in a posh room on the side of the building right next to the CN Tower. If I positioned myself sideways on the bed, I could look out the tall widow at the impossibly tall concrete shaft that rose up and up and up some more to slide through a hoop of lights and glass. A giant finger accepting a ring. I could not help but think about the map of Canada I'd drawn as a kid and how the only structure in the country I could name was the

CN Tower. I assumed for much of my first two decades that I'd most likely never see it in person, and here I was lying in the glow of the tower's flashing lights, shapes and shadows shifting on the wall as I drifted off to sleep.

With the SkyDome looming over me, I walked the streets of downtown Toronto. I grinned when I thought about lying in bed as a kid bugging Bernie with question after question about how high one of these buildings might actually be. I was headed for our sound check at the Horseshoe. I had been there before, to watch the Rheostatics, which was quite likely the first time I had gone to see a band play original songs that I'd not heard before. I remember we had that night off, but we chose not to go to a pub, or to a hockey game, or a movie, but instead I asked around and was told the Rheostatics were amazing and played arty original songs, some that went on for ten and twelve minutes.

"Hmm," I said to my friend Jack. "No traditional songs? No covers? How do they do it? How do they keep everyone's attention?"

I wanted to see how a mainland band did it on the mainland, I suppose.

When Séan and I arrived at the Horseshoe that night you could barely see the walls and floor. It was just a sea of heads and shoulders and twisting and turning chests with bottles of beer pressed to them. The band hit the stage, and for the next two-plus hours I was transfixed. I did not know a single verse or chorus of a single song, and it did not matter one bit.

The experience was so magical that I just assumed the venue in the cold, hard light of day would be equally so. As I approached the legendary music bar on Queen West that day, I passed the place where we'd showcased a few months back. The place where the wind had blown a couple of the letters out of the sign so that by show time it read,

TONIGHT FROM NEWFOUNDLAND
EAT BIG SEA

I walked through the door of the Horseshoe and between the long, narrow bar down one side and a tight row of stand-up tables down the other all the way to the show room in the back. Stickers and band posters covered the walls. It felt a little more roadhouse than I remembered.

I made my way past the somehow-jammed-in-there pool table and paused, preparing myself for the majesty of the show room that had held me transfixed. But with no audience, no band, no coloured lights, it did not look the same. At all.

The wide windowless space was lit with harsh fluorescent lights, and the air of the night before and the night before that still lingered. It may have seemed like just a dim, stark hall. But the back of the bare stage was draped with a black curtain emblazoned with the club's logo, and peeking out from the pipes above I could see the barn doors of a few focused stage lights. A stage waiting for a band. A dance floor waiting for dancers. A music venue waiting for music.

I had to calm myself. I wandered back through the stage door and followed arrows down to the dressing room, which could very well have been called a dressing closet. I guessed it to be about ten feet by five, with a small hockey dressing room bench down one side. From damp concrete floor to stained leaky ceiling, the walls were completely covered with band stickers, Sharpie graffiti, and vandalized band names.

The Skydiggers had been altered to Skyfriggers. Blue Rodeo was changed to Blue Rodehole. The *I* in I Mother Earth was redrawn to look like a stiff . . . you know. When we first saw our name corrupted to Great Big Seamen, we knew we had arrived.

By the time we sound-checked and had everything ready for the show, it was getting close to happy hour, late in the afternoon. By four, the bar was full, and a lineup had started. By the time they opened the doors to the main hall at seven, almost twice the capacity of the Horseshoe Tavern stretched down Queen West.

I walked the line to say hello to a couple of cousins who had made the trip. "Gonna be wicked time tonight." My cousin Mark high-fived me and introduced me to six of his friends he'd brought in from Ajax, where he worked.

"We heard about these kitchen parties," one fella said. "Looks like quite a few others have too. Are you gonna play that 'What Are You At' song?"

I found it so odd to hear Newfoundland phrases said in a Southern Ontario accent.

Back downstairs, you could feel the excitement and sense of occasion building, and then Keith knocked on the frame of the dressing room door not long after eight thirty. "I think we should go, fellas. You got the place rammed here." We followed him up the steps to the backstage area.

We could hear them before we saw them. Some were chanting "Great Big Sea," but most were chanting "New Found Land" when they were not singing "We'll rant and we'll roar like true Newfoundlanders."

"How friggin' lucky are we to have a crowd like this?" I said as we stood on the stage steps.

The place was awash with Newfoundland flags and expat students and homesick cousins and all the mainland friends they could drag with them. We struck the first chord and the crowd cheered and starting singing along. I swear there were Newfoundlanders singing traditional songs from home for the first time in their lives. They sang them for a good time. They sang them because they were their own. They sang them like they needed them.

Newfoundlanders are extremely supportive of each other when we venture onto the mainland for sports, business, and many other pursuits. But I had not completely understood, yet, just how important Newfoundland songs are to Newfoundlanders away from home. More than anything else, songs are the calling card we most cherish. I asked Bob about this recently, and he explained, "We were fellas from home doing the one thing that Newfoundlanders are most proud of—their songs. Music is still the most significant thing to people in Newfoundland. We had a state funeral for a guy who wrote songs. We didn't have it for the hockey player or the politician, but we had a state funeral for a songwriter."

Back downstairs in the dressing room, at intermission, Keith told us that they ran out of every kind of bottled beer about ten minutes into our first set and were waiting on another truckload. After the gig, he would tell us they sold all that as well, and all the rum, vodka, and gin in the building.

"There's some schnapps, and two big yellow bottles of Galliano up there. That's it."

The club manager had never seen anything like it. "It's funny. When a band from Edmonton plays the Horseshoe, we don't get all the Albertans in an hour radius to automatically attend. But Great Big Sea plays the bar and every Newfoundlander for miles is banging down the door at four in the afternoon."

If I close my eyes now, I can picture that night. I can see it from the stage. Not because it was exactly how I'd dreamed it would be, but because it was something no one could have seen coming.

There was a movement afoot. A sense of a secret getting out. A feeling that for a while now a group of people had been spreading out around the country telling Canadians about the place they'd come from. About how different it is. About how hard people are willing to work and play. About how much fun the parties are. About how songs are the most important part of those parties and everybody's got one. And that night, at perhaps the most important show we'd played so far, the truth lived up to the story.

For years after, we held the bar sales record at the Horseshoe. We still might.

CANADA DAY 1997

t was to be a triumphant gig. One that confirmed to the country that a band like Great Big Sea was the real deal, not just a pub band, not just an attraction for folks out East, or even those home-starved Atlantic Canadians at gigs west of Edmonton. We had landed a spot at the Canada Day celebrations on Parliament Hill. Great Big Sea would be sharing the stage with Canada's biggest bands on the nation's 130th birthday in front of an anticipated crowd of more than a hundred thousand people, broadcast live on CBC to millions more across the country, and covered by media from around the world. And as if that was not enough, we would be playing for none other than the Queen of England. The Queen and Prince Philip were to visit Newfoundland for the 500th anniversary of John Cabot's landing, and we would get to play for the Queen herself in the nation's capital.

The Queen and the royal family in general are highly regarded all across Canada, yet they occupy a position of even greater significance in Newfoundland. Not too long ago, Newfoundland was a colony of Great Britain, just like Canada, Australia, and New Zealand. There was a sense, I suppose, that the Queen is not just Canada's Queen generally but Newfoundland's Queen specifically. The royal visit to our island was a serious tip of the hat to our past as a British colony, and having a Newfoundland band play amongst Canada's best was an equally big nod to our present and future as a Canadian province.

This was an important gig for us, and for Newfoundland as well. We hadn't said it aloud, but we were all thinking of how far we'd come. Gone were the four-set nights in pubs with one foot on the stage and one foot on a milk crate. No more driving across Newfoundland in the dead of winter while pulling broken wipers across the windshield with the fiddler's belt. We had become a real, honest-to-God Canadian Band. This gig confirmed it.

We flew into Ottawa towards the end of June and treated ourselves and our significant others to a night out before the work began. We booked a table at a posh restaurant and dined like a team that had just won the championship. That night in our hotel, I lay in bed next to Joanne, my wife-to-be, and confessed to her that I was nervous. "It's all good," she said before drifting off to a contented sleep. I was too restless. I sat on the window ledge looking over the rooftops at the glow coming from the iconic Peace Tower. For the first time, the joy of getting this opportunity was replaced by the cold reality that we had to live up to it.

What if something breaks? What if I forget the words? What if I sing out of tune? What if we blow it? On live TV? We had exactly three minutes and forty-five seconds to perform a song that takes exactly three minutes and forty seconds. If we shagged it up, we'd have nowhere to go, the camera would just stay on us. And then the second our time was up, the show would move on to the next segment and we'd have no chance to make up for the error. I became short of breath thinking about it.

But as dawn crept over the Parliament Buildings, I calmed down enough to enjoy the fact that I had something this big to be nervous about.

As we drove to the rehearsal, I was overcome with the sense that we were going somewhere important to do something important. The stone Parliament Buildings looked both beautiful and intimidating. There were cameras on cranes and lighting towers five storeys high. We were stopped at a security gate for about ten minutes when we had to exit our van and enter a special trailer and have laminated photo IDs processed. We were told we'd have a security briefing with both the RCMP and someone called a protocol officer. The buildings, the security, the cameras were quite a sight for a fella who'd dreamed about all this for pretty much his entire life.

Through it all, I was only interested in one place: the stage. I ran up the huge ramp and onto the wings. The stage itself was bigger than any we'd ever played on. You could have parked a couple of airplanes on it. More towers with speakers and lighting stood five storeys high, and decorated scaffolding framed an enormous covered platform. Stagehands came and went, wheeling in freezer-sized road cases with silver edges and stamped with the names of bands and production companies. A lighting crew stood on the deck with lux meters and spoke into walkie-talkies to technicians high in the rigging above, directing a light beam inch by inch into its required spot. Just about every variation of "check one, two" was blasting out of some speaker somewhere.

As I snuck from the wings to centre stage, the view opened onto the Parliament grounds where the audience would gather. It stretched from the East Block of Parliament to the West Block, from the stage to the street and beyond. I tried to imagine how many softball fields you could fit in this space, but I couldn't. I tried to picture what a hundred thousand and more people would look like there, but I couldn't.

Onstage was a gent in a headset who appeared to be a stand-in for the host, running the lines that would later announce the acts. For a rock band from Ontario, his introduction went something cool like this: "Please welcome one of the great sensations in the Canadian music business!" Or something like that.

Next up was a Québécois chanteuse. Her introduction was in similar style: "From the province of Quebec, we are very lucky to have with us," and on it went.

I knew from the running order that Great Big Sea would be next, so I took a step closer in anticipation. I'm sure I was smiling before he even began. But then he put on a goofy demeanour, and although I could not hear exactly, his scripted intro sounded something like this: "I t'inks I hears a few crabs rolling up the beach! Wait now, dats not crabs! Dats Newfies! Here's Great Big Sea!"

My smile vanished, replaced by confusion. Why was our introduction a joke? And not a good one at that. We had worked so hard for this opportunity, but I did not want to rock the boat or seem ungrateful just as we stepped on the side of the stage.

"What the f—k was that?" I had not noticed Bob was behind me and had heard the whole deal as well. "This is f—king bulls—t."

I convinced him we should go find our trailer and discuss it amongst ourselves rather than storm onto the stage tearing up the stand-ins' scripts in protest. He fired his sun glasses into the audience and stormed off. In the trailer the debate was heated.

"Look," I argued, "we just got here and we're going to look like a bunch of whiners if we starts complaining about the intro stuff right away. Let's get the rehearsal behind us and chat to them later. Maybe we're being too sensitive?"

Bob stood firm. "No, Alan. We are not being too sensitive. This is a line we have to draw and we have to draw it now."

"But I just don't want to seem like a poor sport or someone who can't take a joke." I was desperate to not cause a fuss, but Bob grew even more resolute.

"But we're no joke. Nor is our music. Nor is the place we come from. We have to let them know that a crabs joke is not acceptable or we will be doing a huge disservice to our band and our home. I am not f—king doin' it."

Somewhere in my heart of hearts I knew he was right. And so, just minutes after we had arrived for the gig of a lifetime, I headed off to object to the very people who had brought us there.

I walked through the maze of backstage trailers. There were production assistants with wireless headsets walking and talking while dozens of ponytailed people hurried past with clipboards in hand and cellphones glued to their heads. It all seemed so amazing, so much bigger than anything I'd seen before. This was everything I'd wanted it to be.

I made my way back up to the side of the stage in hopes I might get to chat with the host. On my way up the ramp, though, I was waylaid by a very excited stagehand who introduced himself as Guy. "Hey, there's the Newfie-boy! Come see what we built for your big intro tonight!"

"Oh, I was just going to chat with the host about something." I tried to carry on, but he insisted. He walked me to a back corner of the stage where props and stage flats were stored for the evening performance. "The rock band will appear from behind this bus!" Guy said, pointing to a cartoon cut-out of a tour bus. "And here's your dory!" he exclaimed. "We'll get you four Newfies wearing these yellow sou'wester hats and pull you onstage in this yellow-and-red dory! It will be hilarious!"

I felt the knot in my stomach twist tighter. The intro script with its crab joke was not the worst of it, then. Not by a long shot. "Oh yeah. Um, I really need to see the host or the director or someone."

Guy's expression started to droop. "Is there a problem? You don't like the dory?"

"Yeah, it's a cool dory, man," was all I could think to say, and as I turned away from him I swore I heard him curse at me under his breath. I definitely heard him say to another stagehand that he didn't think I liked the dory. Then they switched to French. I could not understand it completely, but they were not saying how awesome I was, I can guarantee you that.

I made my way to the trailer with an official-looking production sign. Inside, I recognized the stand-in for the host talking with someone about the script. They talked over each other as they waved pages around and pencilled in notes. I stood waiting for a break in their hurried conversation. My palms were sweaty and my mouth was dry. I was seriously considering going back to the dressing room and telling the boys I had spoken up for us. I was reasoning with myself: Didn't getting along with everyone trump everything else? What about being a good sport? What was so wrong about taking a few lumps here and there if it amused other people? That's what we were known for, right? We were not the types to get stuffy about how people portrayed us on national TV, were we?

I certainly did not know the answer. But with some shame I confess to you now that I might have danced with a cod jigger in my mouth and a Dominion Ale in my hand if it got me out of that room one second faster. I wanted nothing to do with this confrontation. I wanted to walk down the trailer steps and walk away. But I didn't.

I took a breath and interrupted the conversation. "Excuse me, I'm Alan from Great Big Sea. Can I talk to you about the intro and the dory?" They turned to face me. "Me and the boys were thinking the crab joke is not cool, and they haven't even seen the dory yet and they're probably gonna freak out when they do, especially if there's any talk of any of us wearing sou'westers onstage, 'cause that's not cool either. Sure why would we have sou'westers on when we're not fishing and it's not even raining, for frig sakes, that's stupid."

Silence.

"Oh, and thanks for having us, by the way."

The look I received I can only describe as puzzled. I glanced around and noticed that everyone else in that trailer had stopped speaking too, and they were all staring at me. Some looked surprised, some shocked, some confused. None looked happy.

The one I took to be a writer broke the silence. "It's a joke. It's supposed to be funny and light-hearted. It's not a big deal."

"Yeah, I know it's supposed to be a joke, and it's the kind of joke we've heard lots of times, and we figure this isn't the place for it, you know. Do you think you could come up with something else?"

"I think the crab joke is funny. Lighten up, man. Have some fun."

"Okay. I tell you what. We'll be fine with you introducing the Newfoundland act as Newfies and making a crab joke if you introduce the Quebec lady as a frog and say 'ribbit, ribbit' a couple of times before you say her name. It's not a big deal, right?"

Every mouth in the place hung open.

One of the production assistants took two steps towards me and pointed to the door. "Get out! Now!" Someone else put his hand on the assistant's chest to keep him from grabbing me by the collar and flinging me down the steps. I'd be lying if I said I was emboldened or brave. I was not. I was afraid. Afraid of getting kicked off the gig. Afraid of offending people. Afraid this dude was going to punt me out on the sidewalk. Afraid of just about everyone and every scenario possible.

"No, I don't want to get out. I want him to answer my question." I pointed to the writer, who I'm sure would have choked me if he could have got away with it.

A woman in the room brought the temperature down a bit. "Alan, I'm sure we can come up with something that suits us all. Give us a few minutes and we'll get back to you."

I turned and walked the few steps out of the trailer. I don't like people being angry with me. I'd spent my young life keeping a happy face on while my older brother and sisters had normal everyday sibling tiffs. I was the joker, the class clown. I was the guy in the band who always raced for the worst seat in the van or the seat on the plane next to the crying baby. But here I was, at the biggest gig of my life, and everybody I'd met so far thought I was an ungrateful, too-big-for-his-boots, hypersensitive, insolent brat who was surely more trouble than he was worth. I could not have been more unhappy.

A young assistant director who must have drawn the short straw caught up with me and asked me to explain the problem again.

"It's just not cool," I explained. "I'm a team player, but we're trying to represent Newfoundland in the best light possible, and dressing up like characters in a Newfie joke book and grinning while a joke from one of those books is being broadcast to the world is not what we figure is the best light possible."

"Can you suggest some other symbol we might use for you guys that you'd be happy with?"

A reasonable question, I figured. Wish I'd been asked it a month before so we could think about it. He could see I was struggling.

"What about a lighthouse?" he suggested. "Everybody likes a lighthouse. You can't tell me you object to lighthouses."

"No, man, I don't object to lighthouses, but—"

"Cool, a lighthouse it is."

I wasn't sure if I'd just agreed to something or not, and I made my way back to the dressing room to report. The boys could tell I was feeling sheepish. They were not. They were ready to dig their heels in even further. Where I saw an awkward moment, they saw a line in the sand. Bob was calm, his logical, level-headed self. "I think we need to tell them we are not using a lighthouse, or a dory, or rubber boots, or cod jiggers, or anything else they might find funny. We are not here to be laughed at."

I couldn't deny it. He was still right. And I was still wrong.

It took me about thirty minutes to find the young assistant director lighthouse fella. "I spoke to the guys and the lighthouse is not going to be cool, either."

"What? I've already got the crew making it! You guys are just being assholes now."

"Well I didn't say I was sure of the lighthouse as a prop. I just said I didn't hate lighthouses. We're still worried it looks like we're saying okay to every Newfie joke book ever printed."

Having thought he had solved the problem, he was now madder than the people in the office had been in the first place. I wanted to crawl under a rock and hide for the next twenty-four hours. When the concert was over and the Queen had left, I'd push back the stone and slither out like the reptile I was.

This could not possibly get any worse. Then it did.

What sounded like a British accent broke my stride. "Excuse me there. Are you Alan from the band from New*found*land?" I nodded. I must have looked a state. "Just a quick word, if you don't mind. I am Duncan Holmesworth. I work in protocol and am in charge of the visit from Her Majesty the Queen."

"Yeah. I mean, yes, uh, I mean, yes sir." I was not entirely sure how to address such a fella but was keen not to make any more enemies. I may have half bowed–half curtsied while speaking. "I'm Alan from Great Big Sea."

His perfectly pressed blazer sported a crest that had some Latin inscription over it that I assumed translated to "Seize the Day" or "In Knowledge We Are One" or "Books Are Wicked" or something like that. The crease in his pants looked sharp enough to shave on. The part in his hair was surely done with a ruler. He opened a beautifully stitched leather binder and drew the cloth bookmark to one side, like the priest used to do with the ribbons of the Bible at Gospel time.

"I just wonder if you'd mind providing some alternative lyrics to the song you'll be playing for Her Majesty." He must have sensed my confusion. "You see, I have been given a copy of the lyrics for the song 'Auntie Mary' and have noted that some of the wording is unsuitable for royal company."

On any other occasion, I would have assumed this a joke, but on this day, I figured anything was possible. "I'm sorry, I really don't understand. Do you find something in 'Auntie Mary' offensive?"

He turned his binder towards me and pointed his expensive-looking pen to a circled part on the lyric sheet of the traditional song in question. "Here, you see? 'Auntie Mary has a canary / up the leg of her *drawers*.' I think you'll agree that such a statement has no place in the presence of royalty, and we'd prefer you provide an alternative lyric."

There have been few times in my life when I can honestly say I was stuck for words. But here in front of Duncan, I mean

Mr. Holmesworth, and his blazer and his crease and his part and his binder, I stood silent. It was only when he tapped his expensive-looking pen on the page again that I snapped out of it.

"I'm sorry, you want me to change the lyrics to 'Auntie Mary'?"

"Yes. Specifically the word 'drawers.' A bawdy reference to undergarments has no place at a royal event. Can you suggest an alternative?"

"No, sir. I can't."

He snapped back, "Very well, we'll provide one for you. 'Aunt Mary has a canary / up the leg of her pantyhose.' I think that works nicely, don't you?"

Surely, I thought, hidden cameras were focused on my stupefied face. I honestly paused a second to give the lovable rogue of a host a chance to pop out of the bushes and say, "Gotcha! You're on *Candid Camera!*"

But Duncan Holmesworth only nodded, repeating his question. "'Pantyhose' works nicely, don't you think?"

"No."

A silence hung in the air like a helicopter about to crash. Mr. Holmesworth was not used to hearing negative answers, I suspected. "I'm sorry, Alan. Perhaps I misheard you. Did you . . . ?"

"You heard correct, uh, I mean correctly, sir. The answer to your question is no."

More silence.

He lifted his blazer sleeve to his mouth and spoke directly into his cuff, secret service style. It was only then I noticed the curly hose going into his left ear. He was on full telecom. He whispered so softly I could not hear what was said, but his body language screamed "we have a problem." His eyes went elsewhere while I assumed he was listening to the response to his distress call.

"Right, Alan. I think we should go to the production office and discuss this further."

My heart sank even lower. I would rather dig a hole from Petty Harbour to South Australia than go back to that same production office where only a very short while ago, someone had to be physically restrained from giving me a poke. When they saw me coming, the source of a second completely new and arguably bigger problem than the first visit, I was sure they would have me escorted right off Parliament Hill.

We walked with purpose back to the production office. The same team was waiting for me. They looked tired now. And just as unhappy to see me as I was to be bringing more trouble through their door. The young assistant director lighthouse fella could not wait to speak first.

"So we understand you won't change a single lyric to accommodate the Queen's request. Aren't you a team player."

I had gone this far, no sense stopping now. I said, "'Auntie Mary' is a centuries-old traditional song. People in Newfoundland have been singing it for generations. If I get on that stage tomorrow, with everyone at home watching their own music finally make it to the big time, and I sing 'up the leg of her pantyhose,' I will have to find a new place to live. There will literally be people lined up Water Street and down Duckworth Street waiting to boot me in the arse. I can't do it."

Duncan's mouth was hanging wide open.

The woman who'd cooled the temperature earlier continued in her reasonable way. "Well, perhaps we could switch the song altogether. Have you play another one."

That would be much easier, and I was eager to mend fences and save some shred of a decent reputation. "I'm really sorry. I would gladly switch the tune to make everyone happy, but here's the rub. The St. Pat's Dancers are joining us onstage and a couple dozen young kids have been practising their steps to this tune and this arrangement for months. I can't go to a bunch of ten-year-olds and ask them to switch on a moment's notice. They'll get confused and upset when their hard work goes for nothing. I'm not embarrassing a bunch of kids from home on TV."

Duncan finally got his mouth working. "This will just not do. I will not go back to Her Majesty—"

"I'm happy to talk to her about it if you like," I offered.

Duncan was so rattled by the suggestion, the woman actually giggled.

"I beg your pardon! You would like an audience with Her Majesty . . ."

"I'm just saying that if Her Majesty has an issue with a song I'm singing, then I'd like to explain myself to her."

"Impossible!" He pulled a handkerchief from his pocket and wiped his frothing mouth. I turned to the director, who was now just shaking her head. Then I thought of another compromise.

"Look," I said. "You guys control the live and TV audio. You've heard the tune. If you mute my vocal when the 'drawers' word comes along, that's your call. It won't go live or to air and I won't be drawn and quartered back home."

And with that, I was dismissed.

My walk back to our dressing room was even lonelier than the one less than an hour before. All the people who were mad at me before were even more mad at me now and there was a whole new bunch of people mad at me, and supposedly one of them was the Queen of England.

The boys were still sour about the dory and the hats, but somehow they'd already heard about the squabble over 'Auntie Mary' and were able to make light of the ridiculousness of it all.

"We're like the Stones on *Ed Sullivan*!" they joked. "Never thought in a million years 'Auntie Mary' would face the same fate as 'Let's Spend the Night Together.'"

After an hour or so we were called to the stage to rehearse and sound-check. I have never felt so cold on a hot day in my life. I was sure everybody in the entire production thought we were nothing but a bunch of sooks. We squeaked out a couple of tunes and skulked away for the night.

On the way to our van, a production assistant intercepted us and asked if we'd be all right with a Newfoundland dog in place of a lighthouse. As Bob had raised a few Newfoundland dogs, we considered this a legitimate symbol for us. It was not until we were pulling away that we realized we'd just agreed to walk onstage in front of a hundred thousand people on live television with a nearly two-hundred-pound animal who could fling the works of us around like dolls on a skipping rope if he got spooked.

That night I lay sleepless again. I explained to Joanne that I was not even sure I wanted to go onstage at all. If someone had presented me there and then in that hotel room with a way to get out of this gig and go home, I would have jumped at it. I am ashamed to admit to it. But it is true.

We arrived on the day of the show like guilty men awaiting sentencing.

The moment we stepped out of our van, a production assistant asked us where we would like them to put the dog we ordered. We asked if the owner could hold him till the show, and the assistant agreed. I have no memory of anyone speaking to us about the problems of the day before. In our dressing room I felt isolated and lonely. We had two shows to do. The first was in the daylight with the Queen and the grand question of the objectionable lyric.

As the song got closer and closer in the show and our turn onstage was just about upon us, I have to say that lightness fell over us in the dressing room. It was just so ridiculous. I watch video footage of it all now, and it looks like we are having a jolly old time. When we come to the "up the leg of her drawers" line, which we all shouted to the high heavens, you can see Darrell and me wink at each other. The whole thing went off just fine and neither the live audience nor the millions watching knew any of the troubles between Duncan and the likes of us.

I had a quick but lovely chat with Her Majesty, and then met the prime minister. Jean Chrétien shook my hand hard and said, "I like-a de colour of your shirt!" I had been wearing a red shirt to celebrate Canada Day, and the prime minister, always campaigning, took it to signal a vote for his Liberal Party.

The nighttime gig went over well enough as we ushered a behemoth of a dog onto and off stage for the introduction. We played the high-energy "Mari-Mac" and the entire hundred-thousand-strong audience sang along in the call and answer. But we got no love from the organizers, who saw us as a bunch of insolent dickheads with chips on our shoulders about, well, everything.

Again, we skulked away as soon as we could. No high-fives, no motorcades.

I was back in the hotel room before the fireworks show started, and when they did, I got up and closed the curtain. As I tried to ignore them lighting up the sky through the sheers, I lay sleepless once more and wondered what had just happened. We'd had a golden opportunity to endear ourselves to the national broadcaster, the federal government, and the friggin' Queen, and had somehow managed to piss them all off.

I doubt anyone would have even known about our backstage strife, but a New Brunswick reporter caught wind of the dispute and found me at a festival a few days later. That's when the story broke and went all over the place. In the next week or so I'd do at least two dozen interviews about the offstage fights with the organizers and a protocol officer. I'd be sick of talking about it in no time at all. One headline read, "Great Big Sea Singer Wants Respect," and the article went on to say: "Great Big Sea's performance in Ottawa on Canada Day included a chance to meet the Queen and showcase the Newfoundland band's traditional-pop repertoire. But the lead singer Doyle is steamed about how promoters portrayed the band as a cliché.

"Doyle said, 'Why is it that Newfoundland culture has to be laughed at? Why do we have to be the gag?'"

The morning following the gig, as we drove out of the city towards another gig, there was much silent reflection. I think we all knew we'd had to take a stand, and as we watched the Peace Tower in Ottawa disappear in the rear-view, we hoped we'd taken the right one. We had to choose between impressing the powers that be or representing our home in the best possible light.

We chose home.

ONTARIO 2

"We can't *still* be in Ontario!" I had just woken from a long nap on the bench of the van and was staring out the window at what appeared to be the same trees and hills and road that flew past us over two hours before. A sign ahead announced Kenora in 948 kilometres.

"Holy frig! How big is this province? This is our sixth day driving across Ontario, and there are still 948 kilometres to go before we hit Manitoba?" I was coming unglued. The claustrophobia of the van was hitting me. We were into our second week crossing Ontario. If I'd had a measuring tape, I would have checked the dimensions of the van, as it seemed to be shrinking by the kilometre.

"Got bad news for you, bud." Darrell did not look up from his Iain Banks novel. "Kenora is still in Ontario."

I dropped my face into my hands and rubbed long and hard. For the first and only time in my life as a touring musician, I wanted—no, needed—a sleeping pill or some other form of narcotic. I would have smoked, drunk, dissolved, ingested, or injected any fruit, vegetable, baked good, herb, plant, or chemical that would have numbed the numbness that had come over me.

Ontario is the only Canadian province you cannot really drive across in a day. Cornwall to Kenora would take you over twenty-two hours of driving time. Add at least another few hours to that if you route through the Toronto area. And trust me, every band that has ever toured Canada routes through the Toronto area.

For Newfoundlanders, or at least for the Newfoundlanders in this van, once you get off the island, there is the thrill of zipping through province after province. In less than a single day we could pass by Nova Scotia, P.E.I., and New Brunswick and be well in sight of Quebec—fast enough to give us a false sense of what to expect crossing the rest of the country. So when I woke up from that bench-nap and realized we were still in Ontario, remembering we'd crossed the Quebec–Ontario border nearly a week before, it felt like a bit of a setback.

On the plus side, on our way towards the western Ontario border there were some great times to be had. Most notably, we'd played in North Bay and I'd met Omer Beland.

I pushed open the stage door at the back of the Capitol Centre near the loading bay. I was after a coffee shop and surveyed the row of shops across the street. The sun reflected off snow-covered cars in the parking lot and the lake just across the road, and it took a few seconds for my eyes to adjust to the light. As they did, I could make out only one storefront sign:

OMER'S VACUUMS AND GUITARS

Guitars and Vacuums! Couldn't really be true, could it?

I wandered across the street and approached the shop. It was on a corner and had tall display windows all around the front and side.

One glance through those windows proved I need never have doubted Omer's multitasking abilities. There on the shelves were new and used vacuum cleaners together with electric and acoustic guitars. An Electrolux and a Fender Strat, a Hoover and a Gibson SG right next to each other with matter-of-fact handwritten descriptions and prices tags.

Past the display shelves I could see more rows of happily mingling guitars and vacuums, along with the odd carpet shampooer and mandolin for good measure. I pushed on the handle and a cheery voice met me before the door closed behind me.

"Hey, man! Seen you walking from the back of the theatre. You must be playing tonight." Behind the main counter of the shop stood a shortish man who I guessed to be in his early sixties, as his dark hair was showing specks of white. "So good to have you here in North Bay, should be a great time for you, really hope you like it, and why not grab a guitar while you're in town, we got something for you here I'm sure, have a look around and let me know if you have any questions, okay, so where are you from?"

Somehow, while stringing six sentences into one, he still managed to smile a smile so big that I could see the corners of it through the thick lenses of his glasses. He held a tiny screwdriver in one hand and was attaching a hose to the insides of a newfangled vacuum without looking down at it once.

He introduced himself as Omer, the owner and operator of the store, and I replied, "I'm Alan Doyle from Petty Harbour, in Newfoundland." As I wandered up and down the aisles, he asked questions about where I was from and what kind of music I played and then he told a story about a friend of his who once toured in a band out East and fell in love with a girl from Newfoundland and stayed out there.

"Maybe you know him?"

This is an awkward moment encountered by most Newfoundlanders abroad. When people find out you're from Newfoundland, they assume you must know their friend who also lives in Newfoundland. You roll your eyes and are about to say, "Dude, Newfoundland is a very big place. I really don't think I know . . . ," but your thoughts are interrupted when the person across from you says the name of his Newfoundland acquaintance.

"His name is Roger. Guitar player."

And then you have to, somewhat reluctantly, nod your head and concede, "Oh, yeah. Roger Murphy. My cousin plays bass with his band now."

I could not help but ask. "Did you ever think it was odd to sell vacuums and guitars together?"

"It never occurred to me, to tell you the truth, but I get some load of people in here because they think the sign is funny. Best thing I ever did." As he spoke, he popped the cover back on the vacuum and plugged it in. It started first flick of the power switch. "Nothing to it, you see? These old Hoovers are the best. Couldn't beat them with a stick. So what kind of guitar you looking for?" As lovely and cordial as he was, there was no denying he was on the job.

"Well, I've always wanted a big cowboy Gibson J-200, but I don't see one on the shelves." I shrugged as I assumed he most certainly would not have one of those rare vintage guitars. But Omer was full of surprises.

"Oh, I keep those ones in the back. One second." And with that he ran to a storage room behind the counter and returned with a beat-up guitar case. He popped it open on the counter. Omer beamed with pride as he showed me the guitar. "A 1972 Gibson J-200. Needs quite a bit of work and has been played a ton, but I bet if you spend a few hundred bucks on it, you would have a beauty."

"Wow." My eyes must have widened as I spoke.

"You've been looking for one for a while, I guess?"

"Sir, me and my father used to sit on Saturday nights and pass his cheap Marlin guitar back and forth while watching Tommy Hunter on TV. Tommy and his guests would have the expensive ones, you know, the Martins and the Gibsons. Me and Dad figured we'd never afford one of them, so we took a pencil and crossed the top of the *l* in his Marlin. I have wanted an old Martin or Gibson ever since, but they're still a bit out of my budget, I'm afraid."

Omer paused for a moment considering something silently until he offered, "Well, Alan Doyle from Petty Harbour, this one is going for $800, but I'll give it to you for half that, as long as you promise to share it with your dad."

We shook hands. He closed the case and slid it across the counter. I gave him two tickets to the show and a shout-out from the stage to tremendous applause.

I bet Omer's Gibson has been on fifty recordings since. It's the best acoustic guitar at the studio in St. John's, and I share it with Dad whenever he wants it. I still play it to this day and think of Omer every time I take it off the stand.

After the show, we went out to celebrate. I tagged along with a stagehand, Ben, who knew the lay of the land. I was happy enough to stay in the local pub, but as the clock ticked towards the dreaded last call, Ben swore he had a far more local treat for me.

"You're from Newfoundland. I hear you guys love a good shed party?"

In truth, shed parties were not much part of life in Petty Harbour. Most of our out-of-house drinking was done on the wharves and in the fishing stores above the salt water. I doubted very much Ben had anything like that to offer, but rather than try to explain the differences between a salt fish store on the Atlantic and a standard subdivision shed, I just nodded with enthusiasm. "Yes, b'y! Loves a shed party."

"Well you ain't seen nothing like the shed party I'm taking you to."

We walked into the snowy North Bay night and turned hard right down the main drag until the commercial street with clothing stores and tattoo parlours came to an end. We turned into what felt like a park, but with the deep snow underfoot and the glow from the streetlights fading, I honestly could not figure where we were going.

The beaten path through the snow got deeper and deeper for a few hundred metres. It narrowed to single file, and I stuck tight on Ben's heels. At one point a breeze sent a ceiling of snow drifting over the path, and for more than a few seconds the stars disappeared and we were in a tunnel with only the tiniest light in the distant opening leading the way.

A few more wisps of snow cover and a twist and turn in the path, and I stepped out into a whole new world. It felt like I had come through a portal and been transported to a new planet. Gone was the glow of the city, lights from windows and street lamps. We stood before a vast, open field covered in snow. Stars in the cloudless sky lit a foot-beaten path that led to what appeared to be a small town. As we trudged closer, the small shanty houses took shape in the darkness. The roofs tipped and leaned one way and another as hazy figures passed behind steamed-up windows. Thin, straight lines of smoke shot up from the shacks' small chimneys.

"Ben, man, this is wild. What are they doing out here?"

Ben stopped and turned with the most puzzled look on his face. "Dude, I thought you of all people would recognize when someone was fishing."

Now I was even more confused. "Fishing? In a field?"

"Dude, this ain't no field. This is the mighty Lake Nipissing!"

We had been walking for *twenty minutes* out onto the frozen lake. My silence must have screamed of a man terrified. The freeze-and-thaw of the typical Newfoundland winter had conditioned me to be extremely cautious. There are so many tales of people, snowmobiles, and even houses falling through the ice. In just the first pages of the Newfoundland folksong canon there are two songs—"Concerning Charlie Horse" and even more famously "Tickle Cove Pond"—that tell the tale of horses hauling sleighs of wood across the ice when it gives way and down they go.

My own sister Kim went through the ice once while we were all skating on a gully just up from our house in Petty Harbour. I would have been about eight years old. Kim would have been eleven, and Bernie, ten. The puck we were shooting around went into a far corner of the gully. Kim went to retrieve it and the ice gave way beneath her. We might have lost her if she hadn't caught the edge. Bernie and I lay down and stretched our hockey sticks out to her and yanked her out of the hole. Ever since, I have been wary of walking, skating, skidooing, or basically doing anything on harbour or lake ice.

In any case, I knew enough to know that being out on the ice was a sketchy proposition at best, even if you knew what you were doing and were familiar with the area and conditions. Here, in front of Ben, I had no such qualifications.

"Don't worry. This ice is three feet thick this time of year. These fellas hauled all this out here weeks ago with trucks and trailers. You could land a 747 on this lake."

I'd never encountered anything like the world we entered then. A mini village of ice-fishing shacks lined up in rows one after the other. Quads and snowmobiles went up and down between them like on a downtown main street. We slipped into one of the shacks, and the heat hit me as if I'd entered a sweat lodge.

Inside, surrounding a ten-inch hole in the ice, was what can only be described as the greatest man cave I have ever seen. Above a fully kitted-out bar next to a dartboard and card table, a colour TV on the wall was tuned to *Hockey Night in Canada*, the third period of the West Coast NHL game. A couple of couches and a few chairs surrounded the hole, and six dudes looked up through the dense smoke as we entered.

"Ben!" they shouted in unison as my guide raised his hands like Rocky on top of the steps.

"Yeah, buds!" Ben caught a tossed beer and opened it in one motion. He handed it to me and caught another almost instantly. "This is Alan from the band from Newfoundland."

"Yes! Newfoundlanders loves a shed party!" The fella I assumed to be the host stood and offered me his hand. "I heard you bought a guitar at Omer's today."

It was well after daylight when I left that shed.

Somewhere between Sault Ste. Marie and Thunder Bay, I looked at the bouncing compass on the dash of the rented minivan. It had been there the entire trip, but I'd never really paid it any attention, as it almost always pointed west. But on this day, the needle pointed almost directly up to the *N*. Foolishly, I'd not taken a moment to notice that the second half of the drive through Ontario does not really take you east to west, as I'd come to expect on the Trans-Canada Highway, but much more south to north. I had not realized how far south we had dipped to get from Toronto down to Niagara Falls and Windsor, nor just how far up we'd come to get to the western half of the province north of the 49th parallel.

Thunder Bay was an oasis. On our long journey across the country, I marked our progress by the signs that thanked us for visiting one province quickly followed by those welcoming us to the next. Thunder Bay was to be our last stop on our way out of Ontario, and I longed to see that sign. And when I saw it, I wondered if it was even real.

"We finally made it to the theatre, b'ys!" we said as we drew up at the stage door of the Thunder Bay theatre, at the end of a lane that would become Paul Shaffer Way, named for David Letterman's famed music director. "We are all class now!"

About twenty minutes into our first set, we broke into our first ballad. This was one of the moments I'd been waiting for. I loved singing ballads, but most of our apprenticeship so far had been in pubs and beer gardens, where it was difficult to put them in a show. You'd work like a dog to get people's attention, get them turned away from the dartboards or pool tables, then break into a ballad—only to send them back to their games or heading for a pee break.

But in a theatre, with a seated, listening crowd, we figured we could get away with a few quiet tunes. We slowly started a waltz, and I closed my eyes to deliver the song with all the emotion I could muster. We crossed the midway of the big chorus and the crowd went wild. Cheers and screams of delight.

I assumed, of course, that they were applauding and cheering for the high note I had just hit, or perhaps for the incredible accuracy with which I played the G or the D chord. I opened my eyes to take it all in. I expected to see girls out of breath and weeping the way they had at Elvis's feet. But that's not what I saw at all. Many of the gals had a hand to their chests and the rest pretended to shield their eyes while clearly peeking between their fingers. Most of the fellas were cheering as if a pal had just won the Stanley

Cup, their arms raised to the heavens. I noticed some of the crowd pointing behind me, their extended fingers tracing from one side of the stage to the other, their eyes open wider than their mouths.

I kept singing, but turned slightly to see what could possibly be taking attention away from this awesome ballad I was singing. I wish I hadn't. A fella was running stark naked right towards me at the middle of the stage, his dangly bits swinging in the stage lighting and making a beeline towards us all. The crowd went wild. He made it to centre stage as the music stopped. I took a knee as he danced a jig for five seconds before a stunned security guard finally made for him. Naked Fella bolted back the way he had come. Last thing I saw were the two pasty-white cheeks of his arse disappearing into the darkness of the wings.

A security guard later told me he chased Naked Fella to the door until he ran into the Thunder Bay cold, naked as a jaybird. Apparently he ran straight to a dumpster in the parking lot and jumped into a cardboard box, kicking the bottom out of it and pulling it up around his waist like a skirt.

The Thunder Bay Streaker had a lasting effect on me. For about a year after, I could not help but look over my shoulder when playing a ballad in a theatre. And to this day, whenever I close my eyes while singing a ballad, trying to place myself on the deck of the ship in the lyric or about to embrace the love of my life for one more time, the romantic movie in my mind is always interrupted by Naked Fella bolting towards me, his dangly bits swinging in the light.

RALPH ON ICE

was jolted awake as the airplane dipped a bit flying over the frozen west coast of Newfoundland. I looked out the window to see frozen lakes and ponds for as far as the eye could see. I'm sure I grinned when I thought of Ben and the boys on the ice in North Bay and how much they would love this place. I might have giggled out loud when we flew over Placentia Bay and I remembered, for the first time since my beer-soaked night on the ice with the boys, that I had told them a few stories about walking, skating, sledding, horseback riding, and other, more outrageous means of transport across a frozen pond or bay in Newfoundland. And as Placentia Bay shone beneath the plane, the picture of me sitting on an overturned plastic bucket in a North Bay shed on the ice came clear to my mind. My hands were waving in full circles as I told them my favourite on-the-ice story, the story of Ralph.

Ralph lived in Swift Current, at the very head of the long-reaching Placentia Bay on the south side of the Avalon Peninsula. From his large living room window he could look out on the long, narrow bay across to Woody Island and the fishing town on it that a few hundred people called home, and where he himself was born and raised. Growing up there, Ralph had watched hundreds of boats coming and going from the wharves in the small harbour, and had dreamed of bigger towns and cities with cars coming and going just like those boats.

"I used to wonder what a car would look like driving around the paths on Woody Island." Ralph giggled and took a sip of Saint-Pierre alcohol. We were sitting in his kitchen. "I wondered how foolish it might be to see one of the old mares towing a load of wood having to pull over to let a big Chev go by.

"Every time a boat would pull near the wharf, a few of the townspeople would walk down single file with curiosity to see who it was and what they had aboard. They'd pick up a coiled rope and toss it down just as the boat was hitting the wharf. Over and over again. That's about all there was to do on Woody Island."

Like so many residents of small fishing posts on islands just off shore, Ralph was resettled in the 1950s—the first of the big changes to come after Newfoundland joined Canada (or Canada joined Newfoundland, as so many still say). He and his family floated a house across the bay and dropped it on the beach in Swift Current, where it sits to this day. For years Ralph worked at the U.S. Armed Forces base in Argentia, the iron ore mines in Labrador, and the logging camps in central Newfoundland. He remembered one year when he went home for the Christmas break.

"Jesus, everyone was home that year. Crowd from the base, another crowd from the longliners, and another crowd who were with me up in Labrador, all down to Dick's Lounge. They must have sold enough beer and rum to float an iceberg. And you wouldn't have to look very far to find one. That year, the cold came so Jesus early and stayed so Jesus long, the bay started freezing not long after Halloween, and by Christmas week, the patches of ice had connected and there was not a spot of open water to be seen anywhere in the bay. It was only by luck I had good studded tires on the little Volkswagen Beetle or I would have never even got her up the road from the house to the lounge. The town, the roads, and the bay all froze solid.

"I was standing at the bar with Junior Lecky and we were sizing up the ice all over the place." Ralph stretched out his arms to animate his story for me. He had a home-brew beer in one hand and a short Legion hall glass of alcohol and Pepsi in the other. "'Jesus, I never seen the bay froze up like this,' Junior says to me. 'I'd say you could drive a truck across that.'

"'I don't know about that, but I'd certainly drive the Beetle across it.' I was only joking at first, but then friggin' Junior started daring me.

"'Go on, Pardy! Even you are not cracked enough to drive on the bay.'

"Well now, I wasn't about to have Junior daring me like that, so I downed my beer and strutted out to the Bug. I stood in front of her and surveyed the sheet of ice stretching out the bay.

"Junior and a gang came up behind me. 'Whadaya think, Pardy? Is it thick enough for ya?'

"'No, b'y,' I said, 'not yet. I should have another drink and perhaps it'll be thick enough then.'

"So back into the lounge we all went, and a drink or two later, Junior started at me again.

"'Go on, Ralph, you got no intention of putting that car on the ice tonight.'

"They all followed me back out again, and I stood there for a second with a beer in my hand and the other leaning on the Bug.

"'Thick enough for you now?' Junior says.

"'Nope. Still not thick enough. Let's have another drink and perhaps it'll be thick enough then.'

"Back in the lounge again, and two drinks later we were back out again with Junior and the whole gang right behind. All hands lit up like Christmas trees by this point. Before they could even ask, I turned to them, downed the rest of my beer, looked over my shoulder at the frozen bay, and shouted, 'Yes, b'y, looks thick enough now!'

"They were hooting and hollering and laughing and pointing when I pulled away from the lounge in the Bug. I stopped at the top of the long, wide grade where countless times I helped a boat in and out of the water. How strange to be in a car on the edge of the slipway. Like being on a horse at the edge of a diving board.

"I was certainly having my doubts, but I was well within sight of the lounge and I could see the whole Jesus place had come out to watch the show. I put her in gear and gunned it down the slip-way. When the front tires hit the ice, the car popped up like it was shot out of a cannon and for brief moment I was airborne. I was delighted to hear the crowd shouting, but not so delighted to think I was gonna crash through the ice when I landed.

"But when I touched down it was as solid as landing on the pavement. I hit the gas and just like that I was driving a car on Placentia Bay. I rolled down the window to hear more of the cheers as I sped across the harbour and made a beeline for Woody Island. As the cheers faded away, there was nothing but white, snow-covered ice and darkness to see, and nothing but the crunch of tires on ice to hear."

"No way dude!" My story was interrupted as one of Ben's buddies opened another beer. "Is this true, for real? The dude drove a Volkswagen Bug onto a bay in Newfoundland? You're shitting us?"

I told them the truth. That I knew several people from the area who were witness to the whole deal. I swore on my mother's grave and continued with Ralph a kilometre or so onto Placentia Bay.

"It was like that for a good two or three minutes, I suppose . . . until it wasn't. Ahead in the glow of the headlights I saw the white ice turn black, and the crunch of the tires was replaced by a slow swish at first and then a full-on splash.

"'Holy sweet Jesus, I'm done for,' I thought. I pushed the gas as hard to the floor as I could and opened the door. If this Bug was going to the bottom, I wasn't going down in it. I drove top speed into the darkness with one hand on the steering wheel, one hand holding the door open, one foot on the gas, and one out the door. I could feel ice-cold water splashing up against my leg.

"Just when I thought I was a fool for sure, I saw in the distance, the tiniest light reflecting in the night. I recognized it instantly as the 'red reflectors on the head of the Woody Island wharf. Jesus Christ, I might make it.

"The car took a dip and I felt the rear tires sink down. I changed gears and up she popped and in a few more seconds I was rounding the turn for the head of the wharf. The ice close to shore was as white and dry and snow-covered as it was back by the slipway, and as I was close enough to crawl to shore if necessary, I closed the door and slowed the car. I wanted to enjoy the last few seconds of the final approach."

By now Ben and his buddies were all standing and drinking to the "superhuman Ralph dude!" As they clinked bottles, I told them the final brush stroke of Ralph's tale on the ice.

"I let the windshield wipers clear the view as I saw the spot where I was born and spent so many days dreaming of James Dean and all the other California movie stars driving around in their cars like big shots. I wanted to be like all of them, for sure, and probably told everyone in town I would be just like them, but I certainly never thought I'd pull a car up to the wharf on Woody Island to prove it.

"I turned starboard, in towards the wharf, and that's when I saw them first. Two or three people from the town, coming down single file. They looked confused and could not make head nor tail of what they were seeing. One scratched his head. Another squinted and mouthed, 'Pardy?!' The third did the only thing he knew to do, I suppose. As the nose of the Bug touched the wharf, he bent down, picked up a coil of rope, and tossed it down to me."

MANITOBA

The man sitting across from me in the van looked nervous. Very nervous. Perhaps he was unsettled because four hairy, dirty, half-starved Newfoundlanders were staring at him like he was supper. Perhaps he was overwhelmed by the smell of smoke blowing in and out on the frigid air through windows that were occasionally all open to the storm. He might have been put off by the smell of sweat and coffee. He was no doubt confused by the dozens upon dozens of half-eaten Cadbury Creme Eggs scattered around him.

I had no idea who he was, but from my vantage point, facing backwards on a deflated air mattress directly behind the driver's seat, I could not stop looking at him in his crisp beige overcoat, cuffs and collar of a neatly pressed dark green suit and white shirt peeking out at the sleeves and neck. I was wearing the same jeans and T-shirt I'd put on two days and two provinces ago. I imagined he must have been a narc, or a special agent of some kind. No doubt carrying some secret in that tidy leather briefcase that he held on to for dear life. His glasses seemed impossibly clean. His hair looked like it might have been washed that day.

Perhaps we should have seen this coming the day before, when we decided to try to make it to Winnipeg for a show at the West End Cultural Centre, despite warnings from everyone around us that an impending snowstorm would render the highway impassable. We scoffed, as any hearty Newfoundlander might, as we figured a prairie snowstorm would be nothing like what we'd grown up with on the ocean.

I can tell you now that we were right. A snowstorm on the prairies is nothing like a coastal snowstorm back home. It is ten times worse.

It is truly a remarkable thing when the highway and the plains that stretch out in every direction are completely covered in snow. To the driver's eye, the road itself looks no different than the roadside or the fields beyond. And when the earth is frozen solid, the road and the roadside and the field can feel identical under the wheels of a vehicle. You might easily drive off the highway and continue on a kilometre or so into a frozen wheat field before you'd even know you'd left the highway. The road, the plains, the sky—all identical pearly white. I was not at all certain where one ended and the other began.

The ride to Winnipeg should have taken five or six hours, but we'd been driving for fourteen and still had another hundred kilometres to go. Somehow, Tony had managed to keep our fifteen-passenger van on the road while strewn around us, dozens of cars were abandoned in the middle of the prairie.

Our mystery man had been staggering along the shoulder like a shipwreck victim crawling his way onto the beach when he waved us down. We stopped the van right in front of him, and I could see he was freezing and a bit freaked out as he jumped in like a man ablaze jumps into a swimming pool.

He thanked us and refused our offers of smokes and chocolate. He seemed so grateful to be in out of the storm that he did not want to be rude and ask obvious questions, such as, "Excuse me, fellas, don't want to look the gift horse in the mouth or anything, but who are you guys, where is the missing bench from this van, why is this dirty, hairy fella sitting on the floor in front of me on a mostly deflated air mattress, and what in the sweet Jesus is up with all the Easter Creme Eggs?"

He was right to be suspicious. The van looked like we'd stolen it sometime ago and had been on the run ever since. When we'd picked it up at a sketchy rental agency in Toronto a few weeks back, we could not, due to some insurance regulation none of us understood, remove the back bench seat of the fifteen-passenger van. We needed floor space for our equipment, merchandise, and our knapsacks, but for some equally baffling reason, we were allowed to take out any other bench. So we took out the front one. We figured we could use the side door to load up instead of the back—not ideal, but we'd make do. We laid out the hard-shell cases on the floor behind the driver where the first bench had been. We stopped at an army-navy store and bought a cheap air mattress to lay over the cases so someone might be able to lie down on it. I figured it would be the closest thing to a bed in the van and volunteered. Good idea in theory, but in practice, the air mattress had a not-so-slow leak, and you'd have to get off it and blow it back up every ten minutes or so. After a couple of days of sucking and blowing myself into a migraine, I gave up on it. A few weeks and a few thousand kilometres later, here I was. A sad clown on a busted balloon.

The place was a mess. Coffee cups spilled their last sips into the footwell by the side door. Discarded plastic wrap from road subs clung to the backs of seats. And there were the aforementioned Creme Eggs. My hands shake a little typing the words. The very mention of them brings on stomach upset and anxiety-inducing flashbacks.

About three weeks previous, we had played a gig at one of the early GBS haunts in Toronto. After the show, I had a few drinks with an old pal who'd recently scored a job as an Ontario region sales representative for the Cadbury company. Dale asked if we'd like some snacks for the road and I said sure and didn't think much more of it.

We were all set to drive off the next morning when the hotel clerk knocked on the van window and asked if I was Mr. Doyle. I nodded, and she pointed back to a cardboard box roughly the size of a goalie's hockey bag sitting in the lobby.

"That's for you. A delivery truck from Cadbury dropped it off early this morning."

It was too heavy to lift, so I pushed it across the lobby floor. I tipped it up into the side door of the van, dropped it on the air mattress, and we sped off.

"What's in it? What's in it?" the b'ys asked before we were even out of the parking lot. We were as excited as kids on Christmas morning.

I busted the box open. "Uh . . . some Easter Creme Eggs." I kept digging and digging, expecting a variety pack of sorts. "And more Creme Eggs."

"What else?" Bob twisted around in the front passenger seat to see.

"Uh . . . it appears, gents, that my pal Dale at Cadbury has given us a box of boxes of Creme Eggs."

When the final tally was done, there were twelve boxes of twenty-four eggs. So, five fellas in a rental van with a missing bench seat and a leaky air mattress spread over guitar cases left Toronto bound for a near-month-long tour to Victoria and back with almost three hundred Easter Creme Eggs.

Like many romances, my relationship with those eggs got off to a promising start. I was enamoured. I could not believe my luck. The perks of being in a band were finally rolling in. I had my first sample with the CN Tower still in plain sight in the rear-view mirror. Sweet, salty chocolate with a tangy, creamy inside. Delicious. I had another one before we hit Hamilton about an hour later. I ate a third one late that night after the gig in Guelph, I believe. As I settled in the hotel bed for a good night's sleep, I reflected on what I had put in my body that day:

3 large coffees
3 small bottles of water
3 cans of beer
1 footlong sub sandwich
3 Cadbury Easter Creme Eggs

The next day I ate two more. On day three, I figured I would not eat any at all, but the drive from Sudbury to Sault Ste. Marie is a long one, and with hunger and boredom setting in, the egg started calling me. Seducing me with its curves and sweetness.

"Just the tip," I said to the egg, and it nodded back to me, I'm certain. But the next thing I knew there was another wrapper on the floor and the egg was gone. The slippery slope tipped hard, and I did not even know I was on it.

A few days later, I hated myself every time I even looked at the box. Every morning I swore, "I will not be tempted by one of those sirens today. No friggin' way. I am better than that!" But the drive from Thunder Bay to Winnipeg is a long one. It was like

The Lord of the Rings, and the egg was the one ring to rule them all. I started as Frodo but was quickly becoming Gollum. I may have even whispered "my precious" as I surrendered to the egg over and over again.

The rest of the guys were no better off, and by the start of week two the cries went up to throw them out before we did lasting damage to ourselves. But we couldn't resist. The eggs were a gift from on high, and it would be ungrateful and wasteful and even bad karma to turn our noses up at them now. By Victoria, we had given out a few boxes to fans and folks panhandling on the street and actually whoever would take them. But we still had over a hundred Easter Creme Eggs in our van. By the time we hit Alberta and Saskatchewan on the trip back, we were revolted by the sight of them, but perhaps like all addicts, we were just not ready to remove the possibility of having a free hit somewhere down the road.

The eggs weren't the only addiction the band was battling in that van.

For many years I was the only non-smoker in Great Big Sea. I'd spent good chunks of my life in smoky bars and dance halls with my uncle Ronnie's band and in the pubs of St. John's as a solo singer, so I would venture to say I second-hand-smoked a pack or two every weekend. But for whatever reason or twist of fate, I never was attracted to cigarettes or cigars or any of it. But as my weakness for the Creme Egg suggests, I could cast no aspersions on the boys for smoking or for not being able to quit any earlier than they did.

The problem for me on those early cross-country tours was that with four or five smokers, there was always someone smoking. Always someone filling the van with smoke or freezing the van to ice with the window open to let the smoke out.

When I first suggested that they all smoke at the same time, the guys were reluctant. We already ate together, drove together, drank together, fought, read, sang, and slept together. The thought of adding one more scheduled group activity was far from appealing. I pleaded with them to come to a compromise, and the compromise we came to was that they would all smoke on the hour and on the half-hour. But within moments there came a quickly growing list of occasions when additional smoking would be permitted. These included but were not limited to:

- any gas station or pee stop, as it would be part of the "stretch your legs" period
- toll booths, as we would have to open the window to pay anyway
- during any stops by highway patrol, as it would kill any other smells that might be lingering in the van
- long suspension bridges or causeways, for reasons that were never made clear to me

We would start a typical drive at ten in the morning with smoke pouring out of open windows. Each of the boys had his own way of smoking. Darrell and Tony savoured every draw of every single cigarette and honestly looked disappointed when they smelt the butt burning. Séan puffed away more casually, while Bob always looked disgusted with himself for even lighting up in the first place and never smoked more than half a cigarette. He'd roll his eyes, shake his head, and make a "pffft" sounds as he chucked two-thirds of a cigarette out the window. This first van smoke of the day would usually end around 10:08 or so.

About twenty minutes later, someone would point excitedly to the digital clock on the dash, which was the only official time signal we accepted. "Two minutes and counting, gentlemen," Darrell might say and open the pack and have the lighter ready for the smoke bell to ring. And at 10:30 exactly, the cigarettes would light and four windows would open to the Canadian elements while driving 120 kilometres on the highway. Most of the second-hand smoke escaped, but a wind tunnel at minus 627 degrees Celsius raced into the van, and as the gents were so delighted to be smoking, they seemed not to notice we were all getting hypothermia.

This freezing period of dancing with cancer would go on till about 10:40, and so the cycle would continue until we reached our destination. Depending on where we were leaving from and where we were arriving, the gents might do away with half a pack of smokes before we even got to the next gig.

"Jesus, this is going to kill me," Tony once worried. "I'd probably only have three or four smokes between Thunder Bay and Winnipeg, and on this schedule, I got nine in me already."

"Well, you don't have to smoke every time everyone else does, do you?" I said to him, but well within earshot of everyone.

Their response was singular. "Yes, we do."

"Jesus, b'ys, have a bit of willpower," I said, oblivious to the fact that I was on that day's Easter Creme Egg #3, with chocolate under my fingernails, a bit of the yolky centre in my hair, my face smeared in white cream, and the wrapper stuck to my T-shirt.

I can only think that in that filthy van, sitting on that deflated air mattress surrounded by candy wrappers and the windows open to the elements to let the smoke of the cigarettes out, our mystery man trying not to stare right at me must have thought I'd hit rock bottom. And I suppose he was right.

We butted our way through the storm to the outskirts of Winnipeg. We practically pushed our van up the ramp into a truck stop with bathrooms and a restaurant. Mystery Man jumped out as soon as the wheels stopped and explained he'd phone someone to pick him up from there. We offered to drive him to his home in the city, but he just held up a hand and shook his head. He ran for his life right back into the same storm he'd so recently fled.

As we inched our way into Winnipeg's city centre, I tried to get a feel for the place, but really all I saw was ice and snow and more ice and more snow. I looked up and down for something familiar. I couldn't find a thing that gave me the slightest impression that we might have a chance in hell of being received well in this frozen landlocked town. There were no sailors here, no seaside, no beaches or wharves or barrels of rum rolling off the gangways. No shanties to sing. No donkeys to ride. I was not at all hopeful.

My earliest introduction to Winnipeg confirmed about all I had heard about it: it was a very cold place in the winter. Growing up on the edge of the windswept, frozen rocks of Newfoundland, I thought I knew cold. "It's so drafty and cold in the house, the water froze on the toilet," I remember one of the men in the woods saying while we were cutting firewood. Another one upped him: "Jesus, sure that's nothing. It's so drafty at our place, the water on the toilet can't freeze 'cause there's too much of a lop on it."

I could not see three feet out the window on this day. We pulled up to the loading door at the West End Cultural Centre. I stepped from the van and my foot almost froze to the ice on the sidewalk. My cheeks instantly stung as a cold such as I had never felt smacked me so hard I almost lost my breath. Unlike the cold at home, it was not brought by wind that blew through the place in gusts. This cold was just there on its own and was going nowhere for a while. It hung in the air and wrapped around you and stuck to your flesh and clothes.

In my road journal that day, I wrote that I felt snow "crunch under my feet for the first time." I recalled an older fisherman in Petty Harbour who used the term "Canada cold." Previous to those first steps in Winnipeg, I assumed this was just another way for Newfoundlanders to differentiate between us and mainlanders. But on this February day, as I stepped onto the snow in Winnipeg, I felt a cold like I had never experienced in my life. In Petty Harbour winters, what lay underfoot was typically a slushy mix of snow, rain, and salt from the roads and fog. Here, though, the snow barely moved when my "because I'm too cool for real winter boots" Doc Martens came down. And every step made a crunching sound of something compacting and compressing rather than breaking or relenting. All the while, my nose stung from the inside out as my very breath froze on the way in and melted on the way out. Canada Cold. I understood. Completely.

"Holy sweet Jaysus!" I shouted. "They must be gonna cancel, b'ys. It's not fit to be out."

We scrambled into our heaviest sweaters, coats, hats, gloves, and anything else we could find to protect us from the cold. We were just about to knock on the loading door when it swung open, pushing the three-foot drift of snow back with it. While we steeled ourselves against the wind, snow, and cold, two fellas and a gal stepped out, zipping up their thin hoodies like they were out for a late-summer stroll.

"You guys are the Newfoundlanders, I guess, eh? So good to have you guys. Lotta people pretty excited. Should be a great night, for sure." They seemed completely oblivious to the storm that had literally shut down a national highway.

Still, I had to ask. "You think the concert will go ahead?"

"Why, something wrong?" The gal slid her hood down off her head, as she was clearly too warm.

I pointed to the sky. "The storm?" I said "The weather? Will people come out in this?" They stared in silence. "Don't you think the snow will keep people home?"

"Oh, sorry, sorry, I follow you now." One of the fellas pushed up the sleeves of his hoodie, reached down for a handful of snow, and tossed it in his mouth for a refresher. "You guys think this is a bit of doozy, eh?"

The other fella chimed in. "This is nothing at all to worry about. Just a little flicker, really. Everybody will just do enough shovelling to get up a proper thirst, I figure."

The gal said, "You guys are probably a bit chilly, I guess, so why don't you just nip inside for a warm-up and we'll grab your gear for you."

And with that, some of the loveliest and heartiest people started carrying our guitars and boxes into what I would come to know as one of the best live music venues in the country in one of the most musical cities in the world.

Growing up, I knew Newfoundland was filled with songs and music. But on this first night, and in the years to come, I would come to learn that if you can't have a great concert in Winnipeg, you might be in the wrong business. The folks in the Peg love just about any kind of music so long as it's played well, and will happily come out when you roll through.

They love listening to music almost as much as they like making it. So just as Newfoundland has traditional songs, and Cape Breton has fiddlers, Winnipeg is way ahead of the curve for internationally successful original music acts. Consider this. The city of Winnipeg and the province of Newfoundland and Labrador have roughly the same population. To my best accounting, Newfoundland and Labrador has produced only one act that has sold more than half a million records.

By comparison, below is a list of just some of the acts from Winnipeg that have sold the same or more.

Randy Bachman
Burton Cummings
Crash Test Dummies
The Guess Who
Harlequin
The Watchmen
Bif Naked
Terry Jacks
Chantal Kreviazuk
Fred Penner
Neil Young

And that does not include award-winning producers like Bob Rock, who to date has sold millions and millions producing acts like Metallica, Mötley Crüe, Michael Bublé, Bryan Adams, Jann Arden, and Van Morrison, just to name a few.

The stereotype of this province being a cold place had proven true, but so much about Manitoba was beyond any description I'd ever heard. She's the sister you think you know everything about, but you really, really don't. Winnipeg, for example, has an appreciation for the arts that does not stop with tunes. Winnipeg is home to its own ballet company, and, I would hazard a guess, forty of the one hundred most beautiful buildings in all of Canada. The Legislative Building with its Golden Boy on top could be a capital building in France or Spain. Its lobby and stairwell are magnificent. I could tell you how high and wide the majestic urinals are in the men's room downstairs, but that would be a bit much, right?

That first night in the city, one after another bundled-up Winnipegger piled in through the front door of the theatre, dusted off the snow, grabbed a drink and a seat if they could find one. They clapped and sang and in no time at all the tables and chairs were pushed to the side and everyone in the place was up dancing. Well, almost everyone.

There was one head that would just not rise. "What's his problem?" I wondered, and made it my mission to get him up too.

We'd just finished our second-to-last song of the first set, with just "Mari-Mac" left to go. I leaned into Darrell. "That bastard is getting up for this one, supposing I got to go down and lift him myself."

"All right," I called, "everybody up! Are you with me!" A roar went through the crowd. The rest of the band was eager to kick into it and exchanged a few hurried "let's go" looks. But I was not to be deterred. The dude was still sitting, a grin on his face that I could not read. Was he daring me? "Well, sir, game on," I thought. I had not pushed a van through the Armageddon of a storm on an exclusive diet of Easter Creme Eggs to get all but one Winnipegger up on his feet.

"We need *everybody* up to make it work. And I mean EVERYBODY." Still he did not rise.

From my vantage point on the right-hand side of the stage, I could just see his head, nodding to the beat the band was thumping under my chants. I knew he was still sitting. Bob, who was in his usual spot far stage left and had a much better view of the fella, was trying to tell me something. He seemed to be encouraging me to leave it alone and get on with the song, but I was having none of it till that dude stood up. Right here. Right now.

"I said we need EVERYBODY up! But we still have one fella on his arse! You're holding up the party. Come on, get up and join the fun." He still did not budge. "I see you, man. Last man sitting! Get with the program, dude!"

A few people over that way shouted something back at me, but in the noise all I could hear was, "Something something something, man. Something something chair."

I shouted, "I know he's still in his chair! Last one in the house. Come on, dude, what's your problem!"

The crowd over on that side got quiet all of a sudden. I saw Bob put his hand up to his face. It was like I'd just told a way too racy joke at a wedding.

"Come on, man. Have a dance." I was trying to steer the train back onto the tracks when the same group over by him shouted again. As the rest of the crowd was quieter now, I could just about make out all of what they were saying.

"Something something can't. Something something wheelchair!"

I leaned into the mic and said, way louder than I needed to, and just as the crowd went silent, "Did you say *wheelchair*?" As the reverb of my words bounced around the hall, the crowd in front of the seated gent parted. There, next to the table against the wall, was a middle-aged man in a wheelchair.

The place was dead silent. Where moments ago there was a joyous momentum that seemed unstoppable, there now was awkward silence as the entire room waited to see if I'd offended this gent.

He looked around and surveyed the room and the band onstage, all staring back at him. Felt like forever. I was about to step to the mic and apologize profusely, which would have zapped the energy in the room for sure, when the fella raised his glass in the air, smiled the biggest smile we'd seen all night, and shouted, "Yes, b'y! I'm from Newfoundland! I'll have a dance with the best of ye!" He downed his drink and spun his wheelchair in a circle as the crowd erupted in applause and cheers. We kicked into "Mari-Mac" right away, lest we tempt fate one more time. By the time the song reached full tempo and volume, our fellow Newfoundlander was in the middle of the dance floor joyfully spinning and doing wheelies with the crowd. We left the stage on heroes' wings.

FRED'S

Across the country or back here at home, the routine was always the same: We'd stop for gas and a wander around the gas station store mindlessly surveying the chips, bars, soft drinks, and cigarettes. None of which we wanted or needed. All of which we'd buy. This ritual would be repeated thousands and thousands of times in years and decades to follow.

Every musician who's ever toured Canada by road knows this ceremony by heart. It starts with an entire carload or vanload of musicians bolting for the bathroom. Once relieved, the musicians scatter and spread around the store and stare in bleary silence at the products on the shelves. To the untrained eye, this might suggest a strong interest in corn chips and DC power adapters, but really the whole dance is designed to satisfy two dire needs of every touring band member. First, to get even just a few feet away from each other, as you've been glued to the same three or four people for at least a few hundred kilometres. And second, to quench the mind's thirst for something, anything, different. You stare at the chip bag or read the instructions on the DC adapter because these things, so mundane, and tedious to most, are incredibly interesting to anyone who's stared at nothing but the blacktop, the yellow line, and the back of your bandmates' heads all the way from Grande Prairie to Regina.

Especially on late-night stops, I wonder how we band zombies must look to the poor nineteen-year-old behind the counter with one finger firmly on the panic button. Four, five, or six tired, sweaty, hairy, dirty fellas sleepwalking through the aisles of the store not saying a word, especially to each other. A gang of dudes, obviously together, but using every second of this visit to find some kind of personal space. I often wonder what the poor kid would say if a local police officer came into the gas station a few hours later and explained there had been a crime, and was just wondering if the kid had seen anything unusual or out of the ordinary. "Any odd characters come through here in the last while?" He'd be diving for the surveillance camera footage pretty quick, I figure.

If you're really lucky, you'll stop at a gas station that has a family-owned store attached to it. It's there you'll meet some interesting folks. And back at home we met quite a few. My favourite, by far, was Fred.

Fred's Place sat on the side of the two-lane Burin Peninsula Highway. It was a little bungalow with faded green clapboard and an equally faded *Pepsi—Fred's Place* sign above a large shop window facing the road and Placentia Bay. It appeared as permanent as the rocky hills behind it, yet at the same time was so weathered and fragile it looked like it might be blown away any minute by the mildest North Atlantic breeze. Like many stores in rural Newfoundland, Fred's Place was the centre of the town's social life, and there was no such thing as a quick visit. That would be just rude, as it was expected that you would converse with Fred and his customers no matter what they were talking about when you walked in, and whether you knew anything about it or not.

I first visited the store on one of the band's earliest trips to Marystown. While the boys had a smoke overlooking the bay, I peeked in through the large window and got a glimpse of the king of Fred's Place. He was a short man, with a jolly shape, and his long white hair and beard made him almost Santa-like. His wire-rimmed, large-lensed glasses fell to the tip of his nose every time he leaned forward. He had one hand on the counter and one on his hip, rubbing what was obviously a sore back, chatting with certainty with a customer.

I pushed open the squeaky door and was in the middle of it all right away.

"Hello, come in, b'y. Now Moses, this young fella here probably got no more time for lowering the crab quota than I do."

Moses turned to me. He wore rubber boots and coveralls, and in his mouth a smoke burned right to the butt. "What do you say about the government bastards, now, out here in their fancy new trucks goin' up and down the shore tormenting honest fishermen here like him and hard-working businessmen like me?"

They both looked at me. Waiting.

"Bastards," I ventured.

"That's right, my son, bunch of lousy bastards, up here telling him what to catch and me when to sell it."

I perused the few shelves of chips, chocolate bars, fishing equipment, and canned goods till Fred and Moses were done their business, and then I turned back to the man himself. It was just the two of us now, so I figured I should start the whole chat over.

"You must be Fred." He nodded and raised an eyebrow that said *obviously*. I continued, "How are you today?"

"Not so bad as I expected to be," Fred replied, with a perfect combination of Newfoundland optimism and complaint.

"Grand day out," I said, placing four bags of Lay's on the counter.

"Yes, we'll pay for this. And what's your name, then? Can't have you knowing me and not knowing you."

"I'm Alan Doyle from Petty Harbour. Heading down to Marystown for a concert tonight with our band, Great Big Sea."

"Oh, a musician going down to Marystown. Well you better get some sleep in the car, 'cause you won't be getting none down there tonight. The draggers are going out tonight so what's left behind will be like a gang let out. You knows what that crowd are like from down that way."

He was joking, for sure, but I could not help but put him on the spot. "My mother is a Pittman from Marystown." I wasn't sure I should fess up, but I loved the place. Always have. It was my Florida as a kid. It was the only place we ever went on vacation. We had tons of cousins our age, and as a teenager, hanging with new kids was thrilling, as I certainly had a pile of time with the same gang in Petty Harbour. Most important, my cousins had friends who were not my cousins, and many of them were girls. What could be better?

Fred wasn't about to stop the chat. "Oh yes, the Pittmans, now they're a lovely crowd. Especially the ladies. Grand, respectable women, for sure. So was Bill your uncle?"

My larger-than-life uncle Bill was sadly killed in a widely reported cement mixer crash a few years past. I nodded.

"And are you one of the Doyles from Petty Harbour that used to be on *All Around the Circle*?"

I told him I was and that my father, Tom, and a few of my uncles, Ron, Jim, and Leonard, were indeed in the band the Boys from Petty Harbour who regularly performed on the CBC's Newfoundland variety show.

"Can I get a Coffee Crisp bar?" I'd noticed the boys finishing their smokes and I was to bring them snacks for the rest of the run.

Fred reached for the chocolate bar behind him and grabbed his lower back again.

"Sore back?" I asked.

Fred pointed to each body area as he spoke. "Yes, Jesus, I got this pain now for a year or more. Started up between my shoulder blades and then travelled down my back, right down past my belt, through my arse, and down towards my tailbone. If it would go another couple of inches, it would be gone altogether."

"You got to watch that or you'll end up in the hospital, I suppose."

Fred turned back and dropped the chocolate bar on the counter like it was a dumbbell. He seemed winded by the whole exercise. "Yes, b'y, that's the truth. And it's no fun in there. I was in hospital for a good while there last fall, with . . . ah . . . what is it they calls it? Oh yes . . . heart failure."

I tried not to raise my eyebrows too high as I paid for the snacks and a few Pepsis from the cooler. I was about to go when Fred spoke again, in a secretive whisper, as though we weren't the only ones in the store.

"Now, I suppose a fella from Petty Harbour like yourself knows the difference in real fresh fish and that old stuff they has at the supermarket."

"Yes, I suppose I can spot a good meal of fresh fish. But the cod moratorium is still making that real hard to find." I was whispering now, too. "You selling some?"

Fred looked shocked. "No! Jesus, no! As you say, fresh codfish is illegal." He paused, then raised both eyebrows. "It's also five dollars a pound if you wants to walk into the back cooler."

I grinned like a fella who'd just made a new friend. "Just rolling down to Marystown for the evening and staying in the motel for the night. Got nowhere to cook it today, but perhaps I'll be back another day and get something off you."

"Yes, for sure. For sure." Fred winked behind his glasses. And then, again with that perfect combination of Newfoundland optimism and complaint, bid me farewell. "Have a good day. Regardless."

SASKATCHEWAN

"I really loved your show. Can I give you a bunny hug?" the attractive RCMP candidate whispered in my ear. My rock and roll dreams were about to come true, I figured. Here in Regina, in the lobby of the hotel that housed the Blarney Stone, an Irish pub that had booked us for a weekend on our first run through Saskatchewan. The pub shared a moving wall with the hotel's ballroom, and on night one, a Thursday, we played to a few dozen people with the pub in its smallest configuration. We must have made an impression, as on Friday, they pushed the wall back a bit to let in the crowd that gathered at the door. By Saturday night the wall was pushed back altogether, and we played to a few hundred people stretched all the way to the back of the ballroom.

The few dozen on Thursday were mostly home-starved New-foundlanders and the friends they cajoled to come get a taste of their mother country. I had not expected to see expat Newfoundlanders on the Prairies, as it is not an oft-trodden path. There is not a pile of jobs here as in northern Alberta or southwestern Ontario, but here they were waving the flag and paving our way into yet another town. It was as if, unbeknownst to us, someone had distributed emissaries out across the country to rally locals for our cause. By now I was starting to believe we might never play a gig anywhere in the land without at least one Newfoundlander in the audience.

I'd had no idea I would see them in every city in the country. I would see them all over the United States, too. We met women from Newfoundland who had married American servicemen and so were eager to expose their families to anything from back home. All across America, there were pockets of Newfoundland professionals who'd been recruited en masse to one place or another: nurses in Florida and California, oil industry profession-als in Texas, and physiotherapists in Iowa City.

It was the same in the U.K., Germany, and Denmark, where there was always at least one Newfoundlander in the crowd lead-ing the chant in "Rant and Roar." I figured the streak would be broken when we were invited to the Shanties Festival in Kraków, Poland. Surely, I figured, there would be no accidental Newfoundlanders there. We were one of the only young North American bands at the festival, and backstage after the finale con-cert, a stream of Polish people gathered to greet us. "Dobra muzyka!" one gent would say and kiss my face. "Alaun," some kind woman would add, "I am enjoying your bahnd still, longer after you finish, as your voices are with me even now." And then, in the midst of the Polish and broken English, rang out, "Deadly, b'ys, that was wicked!" It was a fella in his early twenties. "Buncha Polish people singing 'Lukey's Boat.' Ha! Nothing like it, b'ys. Best kind." And with that, he turned to go.

"Hey, man, wait! Where you from? What are you doing here?"

"From the Brow, b'y!" he said, meaning the high hills over-looking St. John's. "Me and a couple of the b'ys were backpacking in Slovakia and heard ye were playing up here, so ya knows we had to jump on the train. Gotta support the b'ys, right?"

"Jesus, thanks, man. You want a beer or something?"

"No, b'y, no, we got a few girls on the go, and we got to get on the midnight train back across the border. Thanks again, man, that was wicked. Go hard, b'ys!" And he disappeared into a sea of Polish people. He remains my favourite wandering Newfoundlander, living proof that we had an army of people out there spreading the good word.

Back in Regina, Newfoundland students from the university and the RCMP college got word of a good night out, and by the time the weekend was over, we were treated like rock stars, not just stars from the Rock.

Which brings me to the lobby of the Regina hotel signing CDs and standing in front of this beautiful, fit young woman who had offered me a bunny hug, and even though I wasn't sure what kind of hug a bunny hug was, I knew I wanted it.

"Yes, girl. I'd *love* a bunny hug!" I said and closed my eyes and opened my arms and waited for the affection to be heaped upon me.

"What size are you?"

Confused, I opened one eye. "Hmm?" was all I could think to say and made sure I kept my arms wide open. But she did not step in for the embrace I expected. She just stood there with an equally confused look on her face and repeated the question.

I grew more confused but wanted to keep every chance alive that I'd get that hug. "I'd like a large one, I suppose!"

I opened my arms as wide as possible now, and even drew my hands towards myself in a "come on in" kind of motion.

But instead she stepped away. She walked over to a pile of coats and jackets heaped on a table.

"Burned," I said to myself. Shouldn't have opened my arms so wide, I suppose. Looked too anxious, probably. I was convinced she was headed for the door, but she grabbed a hoodie from the table, spun around, and ran back to me.

She held the hoodie out to me. "That'll look good on you and keep you warm for the rest of the trip." She gave me a one-armed hug, pressing the hoodie between us, and then slipped out the door.

"Bunny hug." I turned to see Mike the pub manager, with a big grin on his face. He'd been watching the whole exchange. He pointed to the hoodie. "That's a bunny hug."

"What? That one-arm quick hug and dash?"

"No." He shook the hoodie in my hand. "In Saskatchewan, this is a bunny hug."

That was my first indication that Saskatchewan, like Newfoundland, had a vocabulary of its own. They abbreviate their town names like we do. As I might say "the Pearl" for "Mount Pearl," they say "the Jaw," for Moose Jaw. They have wonderfully colourful ways to describe everyday events. We might say "givin' her" for driving fast; they say "goosing her."

I was somewhat thrilled to hear people refer to their summer homes in the woods as cabins, like we do at home, not cottages like almost everywhere else. Most exciting was to hear that they called lunch "dinner," as I had done my whole life.

It would turn out that Saskatchewan and Newfoundland and Labrador had much in common. I recognized their work-hard, play-hard attitude and survivalist mentality. I got the immediate sense that people here were used to difficult times and solving problems for themselves. There was no waiting on the army to clear the road after a snowstorm. These folks jumped in their tractors, grabbed shovels, and did it themselves. Then had a wicked dance to celebrate the snow clearing. Saskatchewan is the fraternal twin to Newfoundland. Separated at birth. They look nothing alike, but once you get to know them both, it is impossible not to see how many personality traits they have in common.

During that first weekend, the snow came down pretty heavy on the Friday night. "Jeez, Mike," I worried to the pub manager, "I hope the snow don't keep them away tonight. Felt like we got off to such a good start."

"You heard something about a storm?" Mike was legitimately puzzled, while over his shoulder I could see sideways-blowing snow filling the parking spots.

Nothing seemed to faze the Saskatchewan people. "Thanks so much for coming," I said to a table of couples as I made my way around the room between sets.

"Are you kidding? You guys are just what the doctor ordered!" One of the gents tipped his drink to me. "There was a flood in the community hall basement this morning, so we've been down there pumping it out and drying it off. Great to get out for drink after that slop!"

"Oh, sorry to hear about that." I was almost taken aback by his jolly demeanour.

The gent kept tipping his drink. "Not to worry. The hardware store gave us a bunch of those industrial blow heaters. I'm gonna drop in there after the pub closes and double-check on it, but we should be good to go for the kids' parties tomorrow."

I had to keep myself from mouthing "I love you."

I instantly felt a kinship with the people of this place. A place that, at first glance, could not be more dissimilar to my hometown. The landscape and geography of Petty Harbour and Regina are polar opposites. I stood on a bridge spanning the mighty Wascana River and turned a 360-degree circle. Sky. Everywhere. I thought of the thousands of hours I had spent on the bridge in Petty Harbour with my back to the harbour mouth to shield myself from the ocean cold. Facing anywhere but the ocean, four-fifths of all I could see was tall, rocky hills. If I craned my neck enough, I could look up, way up, and maybe catch a glimpse of the flat sky directly above me. Here in Regina, the sky fell over me like a dome. Later, as we rolled to Saskatoon, the sky started at the dash when I looked forward, and beyond the tailgate when I looked back. If I slouched a little, I could see only sky out the van window to my left and across on the right.

"We are swimming in sky," I said to no one in particular. I wondered if the prospect of endless land was any more or less intimidating than endless ocean. Fishermen and farmers both take on the impossible, I figured. Both are better off not knowing just how small they are in the vastness of their workplace, or just how many hurdles will come to make the difficult more difficult. Days, weeks, lifetimes of effort erased by one morning storm. And not a single human thing to be done about it.

The only thing I knew about Saskatoon before I went there was that the Tragically Hip called it the Paris of the Prairies, and having never been to Paris, I had no idea what that could mean. Did it mean they played wicked piano accordion and ate cheese while drinking wine at beautiful cafés? Were the people there French? I didn't think so, but I was honestly ready to expect the unexpected.

After our sound check at Louis' pub at the University of Saskatchewan, I asked the most affable college booker, Christos—who could very well have been the first Greek person I ever met—what Gord and the Hip were on about.

"Have you walked to the river yet?" Christos raised a thick and brilliant black eyebrow.

When I told him I had not, he pointed down a street and sent me to explore.

It was coming on dusk when I turned a corner and came into view of the Saskatchewan River. It does not run through the city so much as it bends and turns and cradles the downtown like a baby in its arm. Silhouetted in the endless prairie sky, three or four beautiful bridges crossed the river as I imagined bridges crossed the Seine. As I dipped lower and closer to the edge of the river, I saw the Bessborough Hotel standing like a palace at a perfect turn in the river on a rise that makes the hotel seem taller than it might actually be. I surveyed the place from the middle of the grandest bridge. The setting sun caught the top of the hotel, the river rolled beneath me and on under silhouetted arches and bridges.

"More like Paris is the Saskatoon of France," I said aloud.

We had a great gig at Louis' pub that night. Some Newfoundlanders had brought along some friends and they in turn were joined by quite a few people from all points east. Many of the students in the crowd were from Halifax or New Brunswick and had seen us at the Lower Deck or at a festival in Saint John. Word was spreading around the country, faster than we could drive across it.

Afterwards, Christos congratulated me on a successful show. "My dearest boy, you guys are going to do well. See you soon. On a stage or in the Elevator."

I lifted an eyebrow. "In the elevator" must be a reference to a networking event with something like an "elevator pitch," I assumed.

Later, I found out for sure. It was well after midnight when I walked back to the hotel after a show. We'd had a great night, and I was hoping to sneak up to my room and get a few hours of sleep before the 5 a.m. lobby call. I went to the front desk and asked the overnight fella for a 4:45 wake-up call.

"Four forty-five?" He raised an eyebrow as though he knew something I did not.

I crossed the lobby and passed a few more revellers and thought I might actually get to sleep without being pulled into the party. I pushed the elevator button and, resisting temptation, buried my head and waited for the doors to open.

The elevator made a pleasant "ding." I had my head down when a crack of light came between my feet and quickly widened. I lifted my eyes and hoped to see an empty elevator, but that was not what met me. Not at all.

"Welcome to Fantasy Elevator!" A dozen or more people shouted their best Ricardo Montalbán imitations as a waft of smoke billowed into the lobby. Music from a battery-operated CD player blasted "We Got the Funk" as I took in a near-impossible sight. There I was amidst a half-dozen dancers in such a rapture that they did not notice the doors had opened. The others were either jammed in and around two large fern plants or draped over two large, ornate wingback chairs. At first count there were three girls and one fella in one chair, and the other was reserved for the Captain of the Ship.

"My dearest boy! Welcome to Fantasy Elevator! So good of you to join us." There holding court was none other than Christos, his white shirt unbuttoned to the belly button, revealing a black hairy chest adorned with a gold chain or two. He was smoking what appeared to be the butt end of a cigar, but I could not say for sure. I have no memory of stepping into the elevator, but when the doors closed, they closed behind me, not in front of me. Fantasy Elevator had a gravity, it seemed. And I was well stuck in its grasp. Christos pulled me to the arm of his chair. "As I explained, my dearest boy, we have a perfect environment of comfort and experience."

The close contact and the sheer ridiculousness of it all made for an instant casting off of any inhibitions. Things had been pilfered from around the hotel to decorate the elevator car: the two chairs, the fern plants, a painting of a ship, an area rug, and a trashcan filled with ice and drinks. A few of the dancers wore nothing more than bathrobes. It was full-on bacchanalia.

The elevator would stop on a floor and some unknowing passengers would be greeted with the *Fantasy Island*-esque shouts. Some ran for their lives—or for their good names, at least—while others jumped aboard and rode for a few floors and jumped off again. Some stayed for the party.

And what a party it was. Singing, dancing, hugging backs and kissing faces as the elevator drifted from floor to floor. Occasionally the elevator would just stop, waiting for instruction. Christos would lean forward, arms outstretched, palms down, to hush the crowd.

"Silence!" he commanded, and we all watched him confirm that the elevator was neither at a desired floor nor heading for one. After a second or two he raised his arms in victory. "We are hovering!"

Newbies like myself looked on confused as the more seasoned revellers took a knee and bowed their heads.

"What's hovering?" I had to ask.

"*Shhhhh*," the kneeling revellers chastised me for breaking their silence.

Christos leaned in. "My dearest boy, the elevator is hovering. Neither rising nor falling. Neither going nor coming. This is a truly sacred time in the Fantasy Elevator and we must pay it respect as we await our next assignment."

A few moments later, the elevator would give a hiss and begin to descend. Christos would hover his finger over the Play button as we waited in perfect silence for the doors to open on the next unsuspecting patrons. The doors would open, the groggy couple would step into what they no doubt assumed was just a rather full elevator, and then Christos would say in his deep baritone, "Welcome to Fantasy Elevator!" He'd hit the Play button and the party would resume full swing.

I must have stayed on that elevator for three or four hours and enjoyed every second of that ever-changing party in a box hung by a cable. By the time the night security kicked us off, the CD player had been replaced by a piano and I was singing and playing. Yes. A piano. Someone asked if I could play, and I said badly, and they said well that's good enough for us. Two fellas got off at the convention floor and wheeled an old upright from a function room into the elevator. What was I supposed to do? Eagles tunes it was, for the next few ups and downs.

Last thing I recall was running to my room, grabbing my knapsack off the pillow, and bolting for the lobby to make the ride to the airport. I had not so much as lain on the bed in that hotel room. I dropped the keys on the counter in front of the overnight fella. He raised the same eyebrow.

"Mr. Doyle. I was just about to call your room. No wake-up call, then?"

"No need," I said. "And no need to even clean the room, man. I never so much as took a pee in there."

I can honestly tell you it was the most fun I've ever had in an elevator and that folks from Saskatchewan rival Newfoundlanders for making something out of nothing.

CAT IN THE CULVERT

looked out the window of the airplane as it flew out over Robin Hood Bay and took a sharp right to begin its westerly approach to St. John's. We passed over the eastern ocean face of Signal Hill, and with daydreams of vast flat plains still dancing in my head, the height and scale of this hill that I'd hiked around dozens of times appeared far greater. The jagged crags of rock seemed sharper and more imposing. It always looked like a challenging hike, but now that I'd walked on the prairies, the Signal Hill trail appeared impassable, the steep steps crawling up the back to Cabot Tower looking like a stretch of the Great Wall of China.

As the plane flew over the Southside Hills, I could see my hometown of Petty Harbour, perched so perfectly and constantly as it ever was. The footprint of the town was practically identical to what it was when I was a kid, the houses just about all in the same places, along with the bridge, the power plant, and the churches. I could even see my house, still there on the same turn in Skinner's Hill right where my own father built it a few decades before.

I could see a boat making its way through the breakwater to head out on the winter water, no doubt to hunt for seabirds. It seemed so tiny in the wide-open sea, like a single farmer plowing a prairie field. Both as wide as the eye can see. Both with no idea how impossible the task they have chosen appears from on high.

Yet they both continue. They make it work. I was delighted to learn that people on the Prairies shared our own willingness, if not eagerness, to problem solve and get it done.

I'd grown up in that culture, of course. I was raised on stories of resilience and ingenuity where men, women, and children alike made the most of what was available to them, no matter how meagre. I had seen dozens if not hundreds of images of houses being floated on the water or being pulled across frozen inlets as tiny villages were resettled to make bigger ones with more government services.

Imagine it. Your neighbour strolls up to you one day and says, "Hey, so we're shutting down this town tomorrow and joining up with that one seven or eight kilometres in the bay. So just pop your house up on a few large logs and we'll roll 'er down to the beach. Then we'll get a loan of a few barrels and tow it up the bay with a few boats. Then we'll roll it up that beach and set it up over there. Best kind."

The fishermen of my childhood jury-rigged every piece of equipment to make it work. They'd carry seaweed and rotting capelin from the shores below me up to the gardens to cheat some potatoes out of the little bit of soil caught in the curves of the rock. The women of Petty Harbour could make supper out of nothing at all and sew or knit any article of clothing you might need by lunchtime. "That woman could knit an arse in a cat" was a favourite saying of mine. It puts me in mind of one of the great-est acts of Newfoundland ingenuity I know of, one I saw with my own eyes when I was about twelve years old in Petty Harbour.

Kevin and Terry, two brothers in their early thirties, had a small shed on one side of the road right next to their house. They were in there constantly, fixing cars and motorcycles and chain-saws and just about anything that made a noise. One day they decided they needed more space and so built a bigger garage on the other side of the road. The new garage was in need of electricity, but the brothers were reluctant to call the Light and Power crowd, hoping to spare themselves the inspections and the like and the money it would no doubt cost them.

"I'm not paying some townie to come out here, now, and run a 220 amp service over there when we already got one here," I overheard Kevin say to Terry as I walked by one summer day. "Frig that, we can do that ourselves for nothing."

"Yes, we'll string it over the house ourselves and drape it on the other roof across the road," Terry proposed. "Just got to be high enough for the garbage truck to get under it."

"No, we can't do that, because the Light and Power crowd will charge us for another service or something. We needs to get it underground, but we can't dig up the road or the council will go cracked altogether."

They rubbed their chins and simultaneously came up with the answer. "The drainpipe!" they shouted in unison.

From out my basement window I watched. About ten feet from the corner of the old shed, down a twisty hole in the recently paved road, was a plastic pipe eight inches in diameter. The local council had put it there to carry excess rainwater under the road and out over the bank instead of over the road where it would erode the pavement in the summer and freeze in the winter.

"Jesus, yes!" Terry held a single finger in the air. "We got a waterproof piece of PVC cable in the shed. There'll never be enough water in that pipe to get through that! We'll just feed it through the pipe under the road and out the other side right into the new garage!"

"Bingo!" shouted Kevin, and he ran and got the long, heavy coil of cable.

They twisted and turned it every which way but could not get it past four of five feet of the pipe. The end was too stiff and would catch in the plastic pipe no matter how they taped or greased it.

Terry was determined. "We'll have to get a leader through the pipe and pull the cable after it. Grab the coil of rope and we'll fish that from one side to the other."

Kevin slid the rope through much farther, but still they could not get it all the way to the other end.

"Yeah, I remember now. There's a little elbow in the pipe, halfway, to turn it downhill a bit and get the water away from the fences. The friggin' rope must be catching there." Terry sat on a beer case and rubbed his chin some more.

"B'y, perhaps we'll call a plumber in from town with one of them snakes for the pipes and have him push that through."

"Oh yes, b'y, Kevin. You knows, now, what some townie plumber is going to say when we asks him to fish a 220 line through a water pipe for us on the sly because we don't want to pay Light and Power to do it for us."

Kevin could only agree and said in frustration, "If I was small enough, I'd crawl through the friggin' thing with a leader meself."

Then the answer walked right in front of them. "Meow."

Boots was an old tomcat that wandered around the hill. I'm not sure if Terry and Kevin owned him or just looked after him, but he was always around. He'd sit in a thin beam of sunlight on a greasy workbench, or climb up the rafters and nestle in the loft for a good vantage on anything he might hunt. And he was good at it. Nothing to see him with a mouse tail hanging out of one side of his mouth and a bird feather out the other.

Kevin ran to the house and got a 100-foot ball of 200-pound fishing line and tied one end of it to Boots's collar. They popped him down the twisty hole with his face towards the pipe. He turned to make a run for it, but one of the brothers chucked a piece of salt fish into the pipe and Boots ran right in after it. The second he was all the way in, Terry put his boot down to block the pipe. Kevin ran to the other side of the road with more fish and called to Boots to come for the rest of his payment.

Boots poked his head out and took the fish from Kevin's hand. Kev gave him a mouthful of fish and a scratch on the head and untied the leader. Thanks to Boots, the end of the fishing line was hanging out one end of the pipe while the ball of it was still safely at the other. The boys had the perfect leader. Five minutes later their cable was through the pipe.

That night I crossed the road and looked into the window of the new garage lit up like a Christmas tree. There were Terry and Kevin and a few other fellas, laughing, no doubt about how they got the power cable through the pipe. Curled on the floor was Boots, happily licking his fishy paws.

ALBERTA

A beautiful tall blonde knelt in front of another beautiful blonde holding her at the waist, their perfect bodies dangerously close to touching. Their firm tummies and belly buttons were naked below Lycra that stretched across their tops and above the very low-cut Lycra pants that hugged their every curve. Their hair was pulled back, revealing long necks leading to perfect faces. Outstretched arms flexed and curled to show muscles and definition. Their long legs ran up and up and up as they moved and bent and twisted and danced before us. Behind this pair stretched another two impossibly tall blondes, one rolling a tight towel over the other's legs and bum while she leaned down to ask if it felt okay. In the distance a half-dozen or more slumbered on pillows and loungers.

This, I'm sure, must read like a twenty-something male's fantasy. But this was no daydream. This was no mirage for five thirsty young Newfoundlanders who'd been lost in a snowy desert for eight hours. This was real, happening before our eyes as we five stood side by side, each with our jaws dropped near to the shiny marble floor of the lobby of the Chateau Lake Louise.

We'd been butting snow for hours up and down the mountains of Alberta through a storm that was well into its second day. We'd scored a gig at the wondrous Chateau. Perched above the edge of the lake, the hotel could very well be a castle in a Disney film, with its high-reaching spires and ornate windows and huge gothic doors. It was quite possibly the most beautiful hotel in all of North America.

When I say we scored a gig there, I should say we scored a sort of gig. Darrell had a buddy, of course, working in the hotel who got us hired to play a staff night out in the pub next to their residence, a short walk from the hotel proper. But we were each to get a room in the main hotel. We could not believe our luck and were not about to let a little snowstorm stop us getting there sometime Monday afternoon. It was slow going up into the mountains, but we made it, a few hours late but eager for a hotel room to call our own for a few hours before the gig and for a bed of our own after.

We rolled through the front gate of the hotel, grabbed our knapsacks, and spilled into the pristine lobby like . . . well, like an unshowered band who'd just driven for eight hours through a snowstorm. One by one we were stopped in our tracks by the most beautiful and fit women we had ever seen. We'd quickly come to learn that over the weekend past, there had been an international downhill ski event. The final was to have been on Sunday, but the race had been postponed until the weather cleared. To our tremendous good fortune, it had not. The Swedish, German, Danish, Norwegian, Swiss, French, Italian, American, and Canadian women's ski teams were all still at the hotel, waiting for their final runs, and with the gym too small to accommodate them all, they had taken to limbering and stretching and massaging in the hotel's lobby.

Newfoundlanders are a talkative bunch, I think it's fair to say. Bands can also be a chatty crowd, especially after a long drive. Newfoundland bands, and certainly our Newfoundland band, would talk the ear off a bronze statue. But I can tell you this with certainty. When we stood in the entrance of that hotel and witnessed what spread out before us, we did not make a single sound for a good minute. Or maybe even ninety seconds. An eternity for the likes of us.

Even when a bellman asked us a second time if we were checking in, all we could do was nod. The spry young man in the hotel uniform had an Australian accent.

"You blokes must be the band for the staff party?"

Nodding.

"I imagine the staff bar will go off tonight."

Nodding.

"I don't think your rooms will be ready, guys, so you might have to wait here in the lobby for a bit."

"That's totally fine!" five Newfoundlanders answered in unison. We sat in the corner of the lobby rubbing our eyes, wondering what unimaginable hardship we must have endured in some former life to have been granted this hour.

A week before, Darrell and I had winked at each other as we passed the *Welcome to Alberta* sign about halfway between Regina and Calgary. "Fresh ground," we said. In no time at all, we were rolling through Medicine Hat and then we reached the Tallest Teepee in the World. I'd seen it in tourist brochures when I was in my mid-teens, but still, this teepee, along with the Saddledome and the mini CN Tower, were the only buildings I knew to look for in the entire province of Alberta. That said,

I knew more about Alberta than most provinces as a young adult, as it had become such a mecca for Newfoundlanders in search of work.

Alberta is Newfoundland's big brother. The one your parents had way before you and who had moved out before you were even born. It is almost a given that you'll go to his place for a while when you get out of school and are just getting started as an adult.

I knew there were towns out west besides the big centres of Calgary and Edmonton, like Lethbridge, Grande Prairie, and of course Fort McMurray, where for many years Newfoundlanders and Labradorians had been heading to work in the oil industry, and in construction and paving, and doing basically everything else boomtowns need. Then with the cod moratorium of 1992, the steady stream became a flood.

"Alberta was desperate for workers, and we are starving for jobs," one fisherman told local media. "So we goes and does what we got to do till the government lets us back on the water where we belongs."

After seven or so hours of flat prairie driving, "Calgary!" was announced from the front of the van. I looked up from my John Irving book and saw the tops of the buildings slowly rising out of the golden fields. I could make out the spire of the building I called the mini CN Tower and knew that it was not far from there to the Saddledome. I had about eight pages left in my chapter. I figured I'd finish it off and enjoy our arrival into the city. I am a slow reader, so eight pages, or about fifteen or twenty minutes, later, I finished my book and stuffed it into my knapsack, preparing myself for a glorious entry into the city that had only a few years before hosted the Winter Olympics. I looked out the window—and to my surprise, the city looked not one bit closer than it had eight pages ago. After nearly twenty minutes of continuous highway driving, the view of the city ahead was unchanged. I rubbed my eyes.

"Did we stop and I missed it?"

"No, Pally," Tony said from behind his mirrored aviator sunglasses, "Welcome to the West. We'll be looking at Calgary for a while before we get there."

I really and truly could not believe my eyes. Think about that for a moment. Have you ever looked at something, then moved thirty kilometres closer to it, looked again and found it looked the same? I certainly had not. Growing up in Petty Harbour, I'd have been lucky to see three kilometres in any direction on land, so I had no experience with the optical illusion that was before me. For the next forty-five minutes I watched as the tiniest, most incremental changes happened in the cityscape before me. It was like someone had taped to the windshield a perfectly trimmed photo of Calgary on the horizon. It would be well over an hour before we could even say we were driving through the outskirts of Calgary, and the outskirts of Calgary stretched on for quite some time. We had been driving in the city of Calgary for what felt like a good thirty minutes before it honestly felt like we were in the midst of it all.

I set out for a walk, anxious to discover the secrets that set the city apart, and I discovered instead that I have an Achilles' heel as a wanderer: I get terribly lost in big cities that are not immediately on a body of water. Calgary is a big city, of well over a million people, and the Bow River does skirt part of the downtown core, but if you are walking in the middle of the downtown, you cannot see the river at all, and if, like me, you grew up and live on a harbour, you can lose your bearings in a landlocked city. I am not totally sure why this is so, but I suspect as a harbour dweller I came to rely on the fact that if I stood with my back to the water, there was really only one place I could go. Or maybe it was a function of having been born and raised in a hilly place. You start at the water and all the town is up. If you are up, just go down and you'll eventually get wet. Easy.

In Calgary I wandered in circles for about three hours, trying to find my way back to the hotel. "It's just the other side of the underpass," I'd tell myself, but I'd walk through the underpass and be at the front door of the Saddledome instead. Another series of wrong turns found me looking at the football stadium in the distance. Finally, I stopped a fella on the street. "Hey, 'scuse me. I'm lost. Looking for the William Hotel."

"Yes, b'y, a Petty Harbour man," he answered in his Southern Shore accent. "Lost, are ya? Wild, isn't it. Drove me cracked too for the first month. Walking around like a chicken with me head cut off looking for a wharf or a beach." He pointed me in the right.

I made it to the hotel just in time to meet the boys in the lobby on their way to the gig. We sang our songs and headed for the hills.

Driving through the mountains is always a humbling experience. Riding below the hills that took millions or billions of years to create makes all my worries, defeats, ambitions, and accomplishments seem so fleeting and small. I wondered if this feeling of humility was how people from the landlocked parts of the world feel when they see the ocean for the first time. As a kid I had taken ocean views for granted and scoffed whenever I'd see tourists parked near the wharf in Petty Harbour just silently staring out to sea. Here I was doing the same thing in the mountains. Lost in thought at the foot of something so much greater than me.

I climbed what I figured was my first mountain near Lake Louise. A nature hike, really, by any true climber's measure. A few of us walked uphill for what felt like three hours. We switched back and forth and back and forth, and each turn afforded a view better than the last. About halfway up I started to sing a bit of a song. I am not sure why. Perhaps I wanted to offer something back to the mountain for having us. Mid-song, the oddest thing happened. I was partway through a verse when I started to feel faint. My vision went hazy, and I felt as though I'd been underwater too long. I gasped, while the others laughed at me. "Jesus Christ! Am I having a heart attack or what?" I wheezed.

"No, b'y," someone said, but I could not tell who, as I could not lift my head for fear of blacking out. "You just got to remember how high up we are."

Someone else joined the laughter. "Yeah, Petty Harbour dogs were built for sea level or lower!"

"It's like there's no air in this air," I said, when I could finally lift my head.

We carried on to the top, and on through the week. I had no idea then that air without air would be nowhere close to the most bizarre experience of my first week in Alberta.

We were blasting through a town in the Badlands. The landscape put me in mind of the Flintstones. You know, how Fred and Barney would be walking or driving and the background would loop behind them: the same tall monolith, the same absence of any vegetation scrolling past every few seconds, followed by the same impossibly perched rock on a high pillar, followed by a valley of dark red clay, and then back again to the monolith. We were in the middle of another eight-hour drive and the van needed gas, the boys needed a smoke, and we all needed food. Again, the only non-smoker in the band, I was free to go to the restaurant counter while the boys and van fuelled up. I was tasked with getting five turkey sandwiches and drinks for the rest of the ride.

I tucked my head into my oversized Montreal Canadiens tuque, with a big bouncy red tassel on top. I wore it constantly on that tour, and it protected my head from the cold and my ears from the constant banter of the van, on the very rare occasion that I was not leading it. I even used the tuque as a smokescreen when the boys were smoking, pulling it down over my face whenever they lit up. I can only imagine how annoying it got for them, trying to enjoy a smoke while I sat amongst them like a very amateur thief, masked in a Habs stocking cap.

With the tassel bouncing in the Alberta sun, I made my way to the store. I wasn't long in the doors before I noticed the tea sets and flags and homemade trinkets that I'd only ever seen in the few Chinese restaurants around St. John's. I also noted that the menu above the takeout counter was half in English, half in Chinese. I made my way past the Coke and Pepsi machines, chocolate bars, and Asian ornaments to the counter. There was a bell with a sign that said "Ring for Service." But no matter how inviting the sign accompanying such bells is, I always feel too pushy or arrogant to ring them. So instead I stood in front of the counter trying to make obvious "I'm here" noises. A cough here, a whistle there, a few bars of a song, anything to avoid ringing the bell. I was midway through a chorus of "The Love Boat" when a short Chinese woman, carrying a couple of boxes and a box cutter, broke through the beads separating the kitchen from the counter. She could barely see over the boxes and did not notice me at first, so I kept singing.

"Oh . . . you here . . . for how long." She must be new to the area, I figured, as her accent was still very thick.

"Just this second, no worries at all, love." Who was I kidding? My accent was thicker than hers.

"Oh. Why you no ring bell? You stealing?" She held up the box cutter.

"No, no. I just wants some turkey sandwiches for me and the b'ys. That's all, I swear." I was ready to bolt for the door.

"Oh, you with those boys?" She tilted her head towards the big shop window.

"Yeah, we're a band from Newfoundland. We've got a concert tonight." I must have sounded honest enough, as she put down the box cutter, though it was still within her reach on the counter.

"I see five boys. You want five sandwiches. Turkey. With lettuce, tomato, and mayonnaise. No cheese." Was she asking or telling? I wasn't sure, so I just nodded. I heard her shout something in Chinese to someone beyond the beads, followed by some hushed conversation between her and a male voice.

I fetched six drinks from the cooler and put them on the counter. The heat was on full blast, so I took off my hat and placed it on the counter as well. In an effort to relax the situation, I decided I should be looking at the trinkets when she came back. I can't say for sure if that's what did the trick, but when she parted the beads again, her demeanour was noticeably more friendly.

"So where you say you boys are from? Finland?"

I walked back towards the counter and could see a Chinese man around her age peeking through the beads from the kitchen.

"No, no, we're from Newfoundland, way over on the east coast of Canada." No sooner had I spoken than a call came from behind the beads, and she immediately retreated for more hushed chat with the kitchen fella. She returned in an even more welcoming mood.

"Oh. So all you boys are from Canada?"

"Yes, my dear."

"Are you married?"

"Me? No, I'm not."

"And those other boys?"

"No, they're not married either."

"Oh. So you all from Canada but none married."

"That's right." I was by this point thoroughly puzzled.

She leaned over the counter in a way that suggested I do the same, so I leaned in close enough to feel her breath on my cheek. "How would you like to make ten thousand dollars?" she whispered, then stood up straight and looked over my shoulder.

"Uh, pardon?"

"How would you like to make ten thousand dollars? Each of you boys." She smiled a salesperson's smile now.

At this point I should remind you, dear reader, that I was getting paid about $325 a week and slept in a half, a third, or a quarter of the cheapest hotel rooms we could find, unless we had to do a night drive, in which case I slept in the van in as much as twenty-five-minute intervals. I had a knapsack with four or five dirty T-shirts and jeans that could stand on their own. Meals were generally some kind of sub sandwich tightly wrapped in cellophane, and of course, a freebie Easter Creme Egg or two. I had no house or apartment or car. I had still never been on what you might call a holiday to a warm climate or beach. I cannot imagine there was more than five hundred dollars in my bank account. So when the woman bent over and offered me a chance at ten grand, my response was quick and simple.

"Yes." I was certain. But I figured I should inquire further out of politeness, if not curiosity. "What do we have to do?"

She was positively warm. "I'll show you." She invited me to move in even closer.

What happened in the next ten seconds left me more disoriented than I'd ever been before or since.

She reached under the counter and pulled out a plastic-covered three-ring photo album, the kind your mom might have had in the seventies. She took one more look over my shoulder to check we were alone before opening the album. On each page, covered in thick transparent plastic, was a photo of a young Asian woman, next to which was a handwritten card with what appeared to be a name, date of birth, and a short paragraph that I assumed described the people in the photos. "All good girls for you. You marry for only one year. They get into Canada and you get ten thousand dollars." She made it sound so easy. Then she leaned in even closer. I felt her lips move against my ear. "No sex if you no want. But they are all pretty, right?"

People overuse the phrase "I didn't see that coming." But I think it's okay to use here. I had no idea how to respond, but I felt I couldn't just dismiss the proposition, as that might be rude. And I wanted to prove that, despite the craziness of the situation and despite my small-town roots, I could be cool with the whole deal. So I forged ahead as casual as a fella from Petty Harbour could possibly be.

"Oh, so these ladies are looking for husbands to sponsor them in the country, type thing? That's cool." I nodded as though I'd been shopping around for such a thing and today might be the day I finally took out the chequebook. "This girl here seems nice. Do you think she'd mind the cold in Newfoundland?" I was desperate to keep the conversation rolling until our sandwiches showed up, at least. "Oh and what about bread, does she eat bread? My mom makes wicked bread."

The woman was on the sell. "These girls are ready for Canada."

"But are they ready for Newfoundland?" I asked quickly.

"What do you mean?" she asked even quicker.

"You know, Newfoundland is far away and that. Lotta fish on the menus. Do you think they'd like fish?"

She raised an eyebrow.

After a few more awkward pitches and responses, the gent finally broke through the beads and laid a plastic bag of sandwiches on the counter. He spoke sternly. "You go and talk to the other boys. Come back with phone numbers."

"Yeah, yeah, sounds good. Let me pay for the gas and this stuff and I'll go chat with the boys." I stuffed the drinks in the sandwich bag and walked back through the store as if I had every intention of returning.

I felt the doorknob in my hand when a shout froze me in my tracks. "Wait!" they called in unison.

Oh, shite. I was had.

"Wait . . . Your hat?" The woman was holding my hat up high and the man was staring me down. The box cutter lay on the counter.

"Oh, cool, thanks. I'll grab it when I come back in a sec."

They both smiled and nodded to each other.

I speed-walked to the van to a chorus of "What took you so long?"

I just said, "Let's go. Quick."

"Why, what's up?" Tony asked.

"Just go!"

"Did you not pay or something? 'Cause I'm not risking jail time over a tank of gas and a few sandwiches."

"Yes, I paid! Go, b'y. Go!"

"Where's your stupid hat?" Darrell said.

"Shag the hat. Just go, for shit sakes."

The boys now comprehended the seriousness of the situation, and we peeled out of the gas station and made for the highway.

I sat stunned amid a chorus of questions asked through mouths filled with turkey sandwiches. After we had travelled what I thought a safe distance, I explained the happenings inside the walls of the Chinese takeout.

Most of the boys were in disbelief. But one, who shall remain nameless, begged in jest for us to turn the van around. "Let me get this straight. I get a bride for a year and they *give* me ten grand? Last time I got married it *cost* me ten grand! Turn this van around. Now!"

He raved about the financial and marital advantages of this arrangement. "B'ys, we'd be doing our part to encourage immigration and cross-cultural understanding and that. We gotta go back."

His last desperate plea was the best. "If we don't turn around, we are a bunch of racists!"

It would take a few more days of driving and gigging before I would see through sleepy eyes a sign in the darkness whipping past the van.

"Fresh ground," Darrell whispered. We shared a silent congratulatory nod as we passed under the highway sign.

Welcome to British Columbia.

FORT MAC BUS

The Fort Mac bus. That's what they call the Air Canada flight from Fort McMurray to St. John's. Depending on the time of year, it stops in Edmonton or Toronto, or both, on the way. The plane, of course, is the same as you might encounter on any domestic Air Canada route: two seats on either side of the aisle at the front, three on either side at the back. There are a pilot and co-pilot, just like any other flight, and the flight attendants are as hospitable as ever, with smiles that seem genuine and uniforms that seem to me to be impossibly pressed for folks living out of a suitcase.

I am a frequent flyer, and even during my earliest trips across the country, the consistency and predictability of passengers heading to and leaving St. John's was noticeable.

On Mondays, the early flights are slammed with businesspeople with one wheelie suitcase and a computer bag they open immediately after takeoff. On Thursdays and Fridays, you see the same gang heading home in the late afternoon. They put their wheelies and computer bags away, have one drink, and fall asleep.

Anytime around Easter, the planes are filled with families heading to Toronto or Montreal for connections to anywhere warm. At Christmastime, the planes are full of university students heading home. Summertime, the planes are filled with tourists eager to get to Newfoundland. Throw in the odd pro or amateur sports team occupying the back half of the plane, and the regular Friday group of Newfoundlander MPs and senators filling up the front after a mad dash across Toronto or Montreal airports trying to make their connection from Ottawa, and you've got a very decent picture of what airplane travel to and from St. John's looks like.

But the Fort Mac bus breaks the mould. I get on the plane early on this Edmonton morning. I watch the plane load up and feel like I know every face. Not the individual people, but the faces. These are the faces of people that don't usually get on any of the flights mentioned above. They are faces from the wharf in Petty Harbour. They are faces that hauled the woods down off the hill in Maddox Cove and loaded the fish truck with a forklift. These are the eyes that used to look out on the bay while mending nets laid over the guardrail to dry in the earliest days of spring, wondering what trap berth they might draw for the summer. These are the lines on the foreheads of men who worried about the wind on the high tide when the last of the icebergs still hung around the fishing grounds. These are the fishermen and sons of fishermen, fish plant workers and sons of fish plant workers, who used to work and most certainly would be working all over the coast of Newfoundland if the inshore cod fishery was not still under the 1992 moratorium. The passengers were all drawn west to work primarily as skilled labourers in the oil industry or the services that support an oil economy. We are the gypsies of the country. Travelling in packs to where the work is and bringing a song and a dance with us and taking a pocketful of money home.

"Second-biggest city in Newfoundland is Fort McMurray!" is a statement you hear often.

A gent who appears to be in his early sixties takes a seat next to me. He is tall and wiry, with not an ounce of fat on him from top to bottom. "Hello," he says. "Name's Bryce." I notice he does not have a magazine, newspaper, or book, and not even a pair of headphones. "Aren't you the young fella from that band?" he turns his *ASPHALT* baseball hat sideways and leans in for a reply.

"Yes, b'y. Alan Doyle is my name. How are you doing." I don't extend my hand, as I figure it would seem too townie.

"Yes, that's right, Doyle from Petty Harbour. Grand to see ye doing so good. Bryce is my name, from Gambo. Heading home now for three weeks to let the wife and youngsters beat the shit out of me. And I'm looking forward to every smack, to tell you the truth."

"You must be up in Fort Mac, are you. Three-weeks-on kind of deal?" I slide my headphones off my head.

"Yeah, just got off night shift now about an hour ago. Went right to the airport and caught the early one. Frig it, I'll sleep on the plane."

I ask Bryce if he's been doing the Fort Mac run for a while.

"This is my fifth year at it, Alan, b'y. Managing the garage for a fleet of the big trucks that goes in and out of the tar sands twenty-four hours a day. I used to manage the garage at the Canadian Tire in Gander, but got laid off when they cut back hours."

Bryce seems the kind of fella who would be unfazed by a tsunami, but to make conversation, I ask, "How do you find it?"

"B'y, I don't mind it at all. Pay is good and the work is good, because they just wants everything to work right and don't care how you got to do it. Grand, because you feel like there's nothing stopping you from doing the right thing for the job. Keep them trucks running like a top and take whatever you needs to do it. They gives you the best kind of bed to sleep in and the best kind of grub. Sure how could you do any better than that."

"Would you rather be working home?"

"Jesus, yes. If there was a job half as good, I'd be home tomorrow. But this is pretty good too, b'y. Three weeks off now. Sure I gets to see the young kids at home more now than when I was working twelve-hour shifts in Gander six days a week. Gone a lot, but home a lot too. Sure it's just like yourself, I s'pose."

"Me?" I was not sure what he meant at all.

"Yeah. Sure how long are you gone working at a time?"

"Around three weeks, and then we takes a few weeks off and goes again."

"And wouldn't you work more concerts in Newfoundland if there was work there for you to do?"

"For sure. I wish more than anything that there was a dozen places on the island we could play once a year. But there's not."

"Yes, that's right." Bryce was nodding with me. "So you gets on a plane every three weeks or so and goes to work on the mainland for three weeks and then you can't wait to get home out of it for a proper slice of your mudder's bread."

"Yes!" I almost shout. "And proper gravy."

"B'y, they're some shocking bad at gravy, aren't they! A bunch of us on the camp bring salt meat with us all the time and shows the mainland cooks how to include it in the Sunday dinners."

"Funny, the stuff you miss, isn't it."

"Now young fella, you're probably as sleepy as me, so I won't keep you up. I hope ye sells a million records. My sister said ye be's on TV the odd time, with Rita MacNeil and that crowd on the CBC. Great stuff. We always had a few Newfoundlanders like John White and Harry Hibbs at the Caribou and the Newfoundland clubs around, but I never thought we see one of our own on the CBC like Tommy Hunter. Well done yourself. We are all proud of ye up in the work camp, that's for sure. A little bit of home we can take with us, I s'pose." Bryce turned his face to the window and fell sound asleep in seconds.

When I arrived home, Joanne picked me up at the airport and immediately asked what was on my mind.

"I suppose I hoped fans would clap for us and we would thank them when they did. But I had no idea a gent like Bryce would tell me he was proud of me, and I had no idea how to respond when he did. I was so grateful and humbled to hear him say it, I did not know what to say."

I still don't.

BRITISH COLUMBIA

was sure I was watching a suicide attempt. Not ten feet in front of me, a man standing on a surfboard was paddling towards the open ocean and what could only be certain death.

I sat on the wharf on Granville Island with my feet dangling over False Creek as the dawn shone its first light through the buildings of Vancouver and out onto English Bay. I was excited to see the other ocean for the first time. Having grown up a few steps from the Atlantic, I figured I knew what seasides looked and felt like, but had been told to expect something completely different when I reached the Pacific.

Impressive as the ocean was, though, my attention was on the tall, fit man disappearing into the abyss. I could not let him do this to himself. I was about to call out "Stop, man. It can't be all that bad," when a woman on a similar board passed close by me. Then two more people. They wore short-legged outfits zipped up the back like thin wetsuits, their bare legs and feet the only things holding them on these boards. As the last of them passed and said a cheery "Good morning! Great day for a paddle!" I began to think they may not be going to the ocean to kill themselves after all. They appeared too eager and happy for that.

Still, I remained alarmed. It seemed they were going onto the ocean for sport.

They were not going to haul fish, collect bait, or empty lobster pots, not going to circle the harbour continuously to bail out the lower holds, or to check a leak, or even to casually catch their supper on a Sunday afternoon. In twenty-plus years of living on the cliffs of a fishing village literally in the spray of the ocean, I must have watched tens of thousands of trips out on the water. But never once had I seen anyone do it just for the fun of it. British Columbia is the very distant cousin that lives far far away and Newfoundland sometimes finds confusing. He goes into the ocean recreationally, and is in way better shape than you ever thought possible.

We had rolled across the border into B.C. well north of here, passing through Jasper National Park headed to Prince George and a last-minute gig at the University of Northern British Columbia. We'd been at a gas station somewhere in Alberta when we were offered the spot as the second opening act for Junkhouse, a Canadian grunge band making quite a stir at the time. It would be a chance to get in front of an audience we wouldn't ordinarily draw on our own.

Bob spun the atlas a few times until we located Prince George. "Where is it?" I asked him. "North of Vancouver?"

Bob looked up over his sunglasses. "*Way* north of Vancouver. We can do it if we start super-early, and right after the gig drive through the night all the way down to Vancouver to make our Saturday gig."

So the plan was to finish our Alberta gig at a pub at two in the morning, sleep till six, and drive for about eight hours through

Jasper National Park and up to Prince George for our 6 p.m. gig. Then we'd drive about nine hours south to Vancouver for an opening slot at the Town Pump. It would be a slog, but the Prince George gig would get us some welcome gas money.

A few days later, we chucked our stuff up onto a stage set up in the courtyard in the middle of campus. The first band, Barstool Prophets, was about to start. Their two electric guitars, bass, and drums were at the ready. We'd be going on between them, a loud rock band, and Junkhouse, an even louder rock band.

"At least we'll stand out," I suggested optimistically to the boys.

"Yeah. Like sore thumbs," Bob answered.

The first band went on, and the half-filled courtyard of clean-cut college kids enjoyed them well enough. I thought we might stand a chance after all, since the crowd seemed in a mood for a great night out. As the Prophets came off the stage, an audio guy rushed over to me, introduced himself as Steve, and asked if we could use the guitar amps and four-piece drum set already on stage.

"No," I said, "we don't need any of that."

"Oh, you got your own amps and drums and stuff? Where?"

"We don't use any amps or drums," I said.

"At all?!"

"Nope. Just four mics across the front and some plug-ins for acoustic instruments. You can strike all the rest if you want."

He didn't move. "So, you're going on in front of the Junkhouse crowd with no electric instruments at all?"

"Yeah. But we got a button accordion, see," was all I could think to say.

Steve puzzled over our printed stage plot. "What's a bodhran?" he asked.

I pointed to the goatskin hand drum on the grass behind the stage.

He nearly giggled. "That's all the drums you have?"

"Yeah, that's it. But we gets people clapping most songs."
I must have seemed like a crazy person to him.

"Right," he said.

I walked around to the side of the stage to reassure myself that
the clean-cut college crowd was still all there. And they were. But
as I turned away I heard the unmistakable sounds of a large bus
or two stopping just outside the gate. Turns out it was four buses.
The first two were filled with sports teams who'd been on a pub
crawl since noon. "Junkhouse! Junkhouse!" they chanted as they
stumbled from the bus and shoved their way to the stage. Judging
from their size, I figured they must play football or rugby and
would own the place before the night was over. But then the third
and fourth buses opened their doors, and out came a bunch of
lumberjackish-looking men.

"Ah, the gents from the work camp just off their shift." Steve
sounded like he was warning me about something.

The men stepped slowly off the bus and strode with purpose
to the front of the stage, the crowd of students and athletes parting
like the Red Sea before them. They opened beers that came out of
nowhere. Shouting for Junkhouse, they looked a lot like the
band's lead singer, Tom Wilson—long hair, beards, checkered
shirts with the sleeves rolled up.

They began air-guitaring and air-drumming to the AC/DC
belting from the speakers between sets. When the guitar solo finished, they just head-banged. In perfect unison. It wasn't long before
the rugby fellas joined them, the entire front-of-stage area quickly
becoming a mosh pit. Every now and again, someone would rise up
from the gang like Lazarus and be lifted to the heavens by the crowd.
They would pass him over the top until he reached the barrier, where
security would escort him to the side and right back into it all.

They were ready for electric guitars and loud drums and songs of angst, not whistles and fiddles and waltzes. They were ready for some serious rock and roll. They were not ready for four happy guys in jean shorts singing folk songs and encouraging them to happily join in the chorus like boy scouts.

I'd not noticed that Steve had slid up beside me. "You sure you don't want to use the amps and drums?"

I slowly shook my head. "No, b'y. Not sure at all."

Back in our dressing room, the mood was ominous, as if we knew we were on a mission that not all of us would survive. "They're going to gut us like a tom cod." I paced back and forth, staring at our set list, wondering what, in the name of God, we could play for forty-five minutes that would satisfy this gang. I made a list of the fastest, loudest songs we knew. Many of them were sailor tunes with bawdy verses we tended to leave out at family events. They would all be in there this afternoon. "What shall we do with a drunken sailor . . ." I blush now thinking of some of those verses.

Steve came to the door like a prison guard leading death row inmates down the Green Mile. "It's time," he said. We headed for the stage as the crowd still chanted for Junkhouse. I suppose they assumed with one opening act done, the headliner would be up next. When the campus programmer hit the stage, the crowd went wild. When he introduced Great Big Sea, they went mild.

Backstage, we formed a circle and gave each other a pep talk. "We did not come this far to go down without a fight," one of us said, while someone else chimed in, "Let's give 'em everything we got and f—k 'em if they don't like it."

"I MIGHT NOT SING THE BEST, BUT I AM GONNA SING THE LOUDEST. I GUARANTEE YOU THAT!" I offered, and with this thin veneer of confidence we ran onstage, Darrell with his acoustic bass, me with my acoustic guitar, Séan with his bodhran, Bob with his button accordion. We started with the fastest jig we knew. I opened with a very aggressive set of power chords on guitar while Séan wailed on the drum. Next in, Darrell added low bass notes as heavy as he could play them. We sounded like an acoustic version of Metallica, and people were digging it. Guys were clapping and nodding their heads in time.

Then the button accordion kicked in.

In an instant the clapping and nodding were replaced with blank stares. Mouths hung open. For a good twenty seconds I could tell a significant portion of the audience thought this was a joke of some kind and were waiting for the real instruments to come out. Bob was blistering into the tune as hard and as fast as I'd ever heard him play, and the audience was looking back at us as if four aliens had landed naked on the stage.

But as we changed from the first to the second jig and the shock of it all wore off, I saw the odd fella nodding again and smiling at the ridiculousness of it all. As more and more beers were raised, we got through the second tune and even got a few in the crowd to sing along with a quick a cappella shanty that followed. Right after that, I ripped into the heavy-funk guitar intro, heavily influenced by the Doobie Brothers' "Long Train Running," of our version of "Drunken Sailor." The rock and roll inspiration and the racy lyrics won over a few more Junkhouse fans, and by the time we played the Barenaked Ladies' cover of Bruce Cockburn's "Lovers in a Dangerous Time," we were not pissing them off that much at all. We even got a few of them to sing "Lukey's Boat."

Our last song was to be "Mari-Mac." Séan screamed like Robert Plant, and we sped up as fast as we possibly could. The crowd sang every call-and-answer part and they even started moshing by the end of it. We said a hearty thank-you as they applauded and we ran for our lives.

I could tell you that we slayed the place. But that would be an outright lie. I could tell you we went over quite well all things considered. But that would be something of an exaggeration. I can tell you, with all honesty, that we did not die up there.

With every step I took from the stage, my smile got wider and wider. Then I smacked right into Tom Wilson, dropping my guitar and pedals at his feet.

He looked down at me as I bent to gather my stuff. "Hey, I'm Tom." His speaking voice was even deeper and more gravelly than his singing voice. He extended a hand to shake, but upon seeing my hands full, laid it on my shoulder. He pulled me in so close I could feel his beard on my face. "You got bigger balls than me getting up in front of this lot with a folk show. But you pulled it off, man. Good on ya."

"Thanks. What a pleasure to meet you. Can't wait to see you guys."

He patted my shoulder and backed up towards the stage. "It's only rock and roll, man."

If you were to ask me if there was one moment when I knew we were going to be successful, I would not respond as might be expected, with a triumph, an occasion when we had been handed a golden opportunity and lived up to it. But as Prince George disappeared in the rear-view mirror, I spoke as frankly as I ever have: "I think we are gonna make it."

"What do you mean?" someone asked.

"If we can play that gig, we can play any gig."

And I meant it.

On the long drive south through the middle of British Columbia, exhaustion crept over us. It was approaching midnight and we had about an eight-hour drive ahead, so we agreed to sleep in shifts to make sure Tony stayed awake. We needn't have worried. The night was so eventful we couldn't have slept through it if we'd tried.

We rode neck and neck with a train as it weaved by us for what felt like an hour through the moonlit night. We stickhandled through a herd of caribou and talked our way through a highway standoff between the Mounties and a First Nations group.

As we drove I figured B.C. seemed to have everything a place could need. Natural resources of just about every kind, and mountains and beaches and rivers and lakes. But I was focused on one thing. The Pacific Ocean. I was not even sure why, but I was compelled to touch it. Perhaps I figured then, and not until then, could I finally say that I'd sung my way across the country.

Dawn was just about to creep into the van when I finally fell asleep for an hour or so, and when I woke we were rolling across the impressive bridge and into Vancouver. It was still very early, and we wouldn't be able to get into our room at the hotel for quite some time, so I walked the streets and discovered Granville Island. I walked to the wharf and there it was. The Pacific Ocean. The other side of the country. I climbed down a ladder and reached into the water. It was warmer than I expected and I let it wash over my hand for a moment. I climbed back up and was about to reflect on it all when I was interrupted by and a man on a surfboard.

As the paddler disappeared out of sight, I turned my attention back to the city. By now the light of day beamed upon it. Vancouver is a big city. A really big city. Right on the ocean. Before Vancouver, Halifax would have been the biggest city on the ocean I'd seen, only Halifax is about a tenth as big. And as the morning sun hit high-rise apartment buildings and ten-storey-high bridges with lanes of highway traffic, Halifax and home felt half a world away. And I was not all that wrong.

Wide awake on one of the overnight drives across the country, I had taken the map and studied the distances in a table. Sitting on the wharf here on Granville Island, I was farther away from Petty Harbour than if I was in Dublin, or London, or Paris, or Copenhagen. Petty Harbour to Vancouver, B.C., is about the same distance as Petty Harbour to Berlin. Gambia is closer to my house than Tofino.

I got up and wandered the streets, excited and exhausted, feeling a confusing mix of accomplishment and homesickness. I came to a payphone. I quickly did the time conversion in my head and realized dawn in Vancouver would be near noon back home in Petty Harbour. I reached into my pocket and found my long-distance calling card, punched in about three thousand digits, heard the phone ring, and heard Dad's voice say, "Hello."

"Hey, Dad."

"What are ya at, my son? Where are you to?"

"I'm in Vancouver."

"Ah yes. Out West. Great stuff. Here's your mother." I could tell there was probably dinner on the go so Dad was not wasting any time chatting.

"Alan, honey, how are you? Have you got lots to eat?"

"Yeah, Mom, lots to eat." I could picture her in her warrior pose in the kitchen. After a few more questions about cousins I should see somewhere out here, she said, "Bernie's upstairs and wants to talk to you."

My brother had taken the fancy new cordless phone and was sitting on the bed in our old room. The same room where I'd peppered him with endless questions about everything and everywhere.

"Hey man, how are you finding B.C.?"

"All good. In Vancouver, one gig here tonight and then we start the long trip back."

"Vancouver. Yes, b'y." Bernie stood up—I could hear the familiar creak of the mattress. "How far away is that, Al?" I knew he was kidding, but I could not help but answer.

"Vancouver is exactly 5018 kilometres away, Bern." We shared a laugh, and I knew he wanted to get downstairs to the gravy. "Anyway, I'm pretty bagged, as we drove all night. Heading to the hotel for a nap. But it's all good. Gigs are going great. Even did well with the Junkhouse gang last night. I think we are gonna make it."

As I looked over the skyline of Vancouver, Bernie's reply was certain.

"You already have."

HOME AGAIN

On one of the last mornings in February of 2002, I drove Joanne to work. When she jumped out of her seat, on cue our mixed breed, Molly, jumped from the back seat into the front passenger seat before Joanne could even get the door closed. She would start whining with excitement before we got to the Cuckold's Cove Trail, knowing it was her time off leash, dashing off the groomed path through the brush and woods on the way up to Signal Hill and the reward of a vista of nothing but open sea.

Molly was grateful for this routine, the way that dogs appreciate all things equally. And I was grateful that I managed to maintain it whenever I was home.

Later that morning the phone rang. I got up from the kitchen stool at the counter overlooking St. John's harbour and answered.

"Hello, Alan, Garry Newman here. Good morning to you."

The president of Warner Music Canada was calling my house. I stood a little straighter as I answered. "Oh hey, Garry. Cheers from Newfoundland. I'm good. How are you?"

"I'm great today, Alan, because I'm calling to congratulate you. You've got the number one record in the country, son."

"What?"

"Yes sir, you beat out a few international releases and a bunch of domestic ones, too." And then he said something that I'll never forget. "Newfoundland is loved from coast to coast."

"Oh yeah?"

"Yes sir. You guys and Newfoundland and Newfoundland music are the hottest thing in the country. They love you in Halifax and all the way to Victoria and back."

After he hung up, I thought about what he had said. There once had been Newfie joke books in stores, now there were classy Newfoundland tourism posters along the Gardiner Expressway into downtown Toronto. A while back, Newfoundlanders had been trying to mask their accents in Alberta, and now many Albertans were jumping at the chance to explain that they had Newfoundland roots. Without actually knowing it was happening, Newfoundland had become not just welcomed, accepted, and understood, but popular, even fashionable. From a punchline to beloved in less than a decade. And we were along for that ride.

Not too long after that I was in a taxi in Toronto when a Great Big Sea song came on the radio, just after a tune by Our Lady Peace and just before a classic from Céline Dion and a percussive track from Susan Aglukark. I turned to the record label rep accompanying me. "One of the biggest radio stations in the country just played, back to back to back to back, an urban rock band, a traditional Celtic group, a French pop diva, and an Inuk singer-songwriter. What a place. I doubt there is another country in the world where that is even remotely possible."

He nodded. "Amazing, isn't it!"

A few years later, the invitation came from Parliament Hill.

It would be our first visit back since the now infamous gig of 1997. Another chance to represent Newfoundland on the Hill on Canada Day. Another chance to play in front of royalty, no less, only this time it would be Prince William and his new bride.

And this time the organizers were delighted to have a Newfoundland band on the bill. The show-time introductions had an easy humour to them, but they were also classy and respectful. No crab jokes. No one making fun of our dialect. Not a sou'wester in sight. And no visits from protocol officers to change the lyrics of a Newfoundland traditional song. As a matter of fact, the heirs to the British Crown stood with the crowd during "Lukey's Boat" and sang "Aha me boys a riddle I day."

O Canada.

Back at home in St John's, I was being interviewed by a local paper with a bit of a republican Newfoundland bent. The interviewer himself was a staunch supporter of a return to independence, and his sentiments were not that far removed from those of my fore-fathers. His first question was, "How are you?" His second was, "So you've left and gone up to Canada a few times?" And his third was, "How has the Canadian Wolf been treating you?"

I chuckled. "Ha! Quite well, sir. I have not been everywhere in Canada yet. I can't wait for the chance to explore up north and more of Quebec, but I'm grateful for how we've been welcomed so far. From the gang on CBC's *This Hour Has 22 Minutes*, to the likes of Christopher Pratt in the National Gallery, to bands like ourselves, it feels like a good time to be a Newfoundlander."

He was particularly interested in how I saw Newfoundland's place at the Canadian supper table, as he put it. I told him about our hit CD, being played on the Toronto radio station, and the welcome we'd just had at Parliament Hill. I explained how proud

I was to have our people's culture as embraced as anyone else's. "Well, I s'pose at the Canadian supper table, Newfoundland is a newly adopted son, and I am so proud to call Canada my home," I said. I figured that would be the end of the line of questioning.

The interviewer looked terribly unimpressed. I don't think he even wrote down my response. He leaned in and asked something I'd never been asked before: "So what are you? A Newfoundlander or a Canadian?"

I was caught off guard and had to think about it for a moment. "My parents were born in the 1940s in a place called Newfoundland. About twenty years later, I was born in the same place as them, but by then it was called Newfoundland, Canada. As a young person, I wondered if Newfoundland and Canada were really two separate places. Now, as an adult, I am very happy to tell you that they are not. Just like so many other cultures and races, mine has been welcomed, and celebrated at the Canadian supper table.

"I have been welcomed and delighted to learn I don't have to choose to be a Newfoundlander or Canadian, because I am both.

"I am a Canadian from Newfoundland. I am a Newfoundlander in Canada."

ACKNOWLEDGEMENTS

I am grateful to my long-time collaborator Bob Hallett for remembering what I could not and for helping me with this project from start to finish. Likewise, Stephen Brunt offered advice and counsel in the earliest stages of writing this book that proved invaluable.

Thanks to all at Doubleday Canada, especially Martha Kanya-Forstner, Ward Hawkes, Kelly Hill, and Scott Sellers for the editing, fact checking, design, and marketing, respectively.

Michael Levine, my literary agent, once again, amazes me in his ability to connect people and ideas. His full contribution to the arts in Canada is staggering.

I am forever grateful to my manager, Louis Thomas, and all at Sonic Entertainment in Halifax for giving so much of their time and talents to the likes of me for so, so long.

Much love to my Jean and Tom, my mom and dad. A million thanks to my brother, Bernie, my sisters, Kim and Michelle, and to their wonderful families.

All the love in the world to my beautiful wife, Joanne, and my beautiful son, Henry.

Finally, to the fans and friends who give me a life on stage and in songs and stories, I am more grateful to you than I can ever say.

ALAN DOYLE is a Canadian musician, actor, and writer. His albums as a solo artist and as front man for the Newfoundland Celtic-rock band Great Big Sea have sold over a million copies, and he has starred in such features as Ridley Scott's *Robin Hood* and CBC's *Republic of Doyle*. His first book, *Where I Belong*, published in 2014, was a national bestseller. Alan lives in St. John's, Newfoundland.